INSTRUCTOR'S

to accompany

WILD GOOSE MARINA, INC.

Second Edition

Sales, Service, and Moorage of Houseboats

A COMPUTERIZED BUSINESS SIMULATION

Leland E. Mansuetti
Keith L. Weidkamp
Both of Sierra College

IRWIN

Chicago • Bogotá • Boston • Buenos Aires • Caracas
London • Madrid • Mexico City • Sydney • Toronto

Richard D. Irwin, makes no warranties, either expressed or implied, regarding the enclosed computer software package, its merchantability, or its fitness for any particular purpose. The exclusion of implied warranties is not permitted by some states. The exclusion may not apply to you. This warranty provides you with specific legal rights. There may be other rights that you may have which may vary from state to state. © Richard D. Irwin, 1990

© Richard D. Irwin, a Times Mirror Higher Education Group, Inc. company, 1993 and 1996

All rights reserved. The contents, or parts thereof, may be reproduced for classroom use with *Wild Goose Marina, Inc.,* Second Edition, by Mansuetti and Weidkamp, provided such reproductions bear copyright notice and the number reproduced does not exceed the number of students using the text, but may not be reproduced in any form for any other purpose without written permission of the publisher.

IBM and IBM PC are registered trademarks of International Business Machines Corporation.

Printed in the United States of America.

ISBN 0-256-14010-3

1 2 3 4 5 6 7 8 9 0 WCB 3 2 1 0 9 8 7 6

TABLE OF CONTENTS

INTRODUCTION 1

INSTRUCTOR INFORMATION 3

    When To Use the Wild Goose Marina Practice Set 4

    Hardware and Software Requirements 4

    Software and Student Handbook Features 4

    Completion Time and Special Student Instructions 5

    What Students Need To Remember 6

    Making Copies or Backup Diskettes 7

    "Viruses" 8

    Using the Reset Disk 8

    Using the FINDNAME Program 9

    Error Messages 10

    Loading the Program to a Hard Disk Drive 11

    Student's Personal Computer with a Hard Disk Drive 11

    Black and White Monitors 12

    Faculty Service 12

STUDENT DOCUMENTS FOR JUNE 1-8 13

STUDENT DOCUMENTS FOR JUNE 9-15 21

MID-PROJECT EVALUATION, WILD GOOSE MARINA, INC., JUNE 15, 1997 39

STUDENT DOCUMENTS FOR JUNE 16-22 47

STUDENT DOCUMENTS FOR THE WEEK OF JUNE 23-30 53
FINAL STUDENT DOCUMENTS FOR THE END OF THE SECOND QUARTER, JUNE 30, 1997 61

FINAL EVALUATION, WILD GOOSE MARINA, INC., JUNE 30, 1997 93

OPTIONAL PROBLEMS 105

INTRODUCTION

The **Wild Goose Marina, Incorporated**, computerized practice set has been designed with two important objectives in mind. First and foremost, the student will receive a thorough review of all the major accounting concepts found in Financial Accounting and in the introduction to Intermediate Accounting. While reviewing these concepts, the student will become familiar with a computerized accounting system similar to commercial systems found in the business world. The computer will quickly and efficiently take care of all of the time consuming bookkeeping tasks and statement preparation and give the student time for statement evaluation and decision making.

Sophisticated, yet easy to use, software will allow the student to work very rapidly and efficiently through a variety of business transactions. At the end of each accounting session (7-8 days/22-30 transactions) the student will find a convenient **"Check It Out"** block to compare account balances and trial balance totals. If errors are found, the student will simply follow the audit trail provided, locate the errors, and then make the necessary corrections. **Mid-project** (June 15) and **final-project evaluations** (June 30, the end of the second quarter) will be performed by printing selected documents and answering a series of analytical questions. This process will provide a detailed review of the financial information. Time originally spent preparing the documents will now be spent evaluating the statements and the business operations.

The Wild Goose Marina, Inc., accounting system is menu driven. Data entry is accomplished using a general journal screen for journalizing and validation. A pull down screen for the chart of accounts and automatic journalizing is accessible with a single keystroke (**F1 Key**). The amount of the credit entry can be automatically entered using the **F10 Key**. A customer and vendor list will automatically appear when the Accounts Receivable account or the Accounts Payable account is a part of the journal entry. Printing documents for review and analysis is quick and easy. All ledgers and the journal (all or part) can also be brought to the screen for quick review.

A **special feature** of the practice set is the **automatic closing process** option which allows the student to close the books quickly and efficiently with a single keystroke. The closing entry procedure, which is so time consuming when completed manually, is similar to many commercial systems. A **reinstatement option** allows the student to reopen the accounts, if necessary, for error correction purposes.

The overall objective of this practice set is to provide students an opportunity to use, learn, and review a tremendous amount of financial/corporate accounting information, transactions, and financial documents in a very short period of time. Using this computerized accounting system allows the students to fully realize this objective, maximize their study time, and to move closer to the real world accounting environment.

The **Instructor's Reset Disk** provided with this manual provides the instructor a valuable feature similar to a real world backup accounting system. This disk can be used to "rescue" students and make their computer exposure a positive accounting learning experience. The reset disk will allow the instructor to reset a student disk back to the beginning of the period, or to the end of any data entry session. This will simplify problems incurred with damaged disks or malfunctioning hardware.

A new "student proof" protection system on the student program disk makes it impossible to transfer data files or to move a name file from one disk to another *WITHOUT DETECTION*. Attempts to alter a student disk will result in the student disk being unusable. An error message that says, "NAME CORRUPT" will appear on any student program disk where a file change has been attempted. A special "FINDNAME" program included on the instructor's disk will allow the instructor to examine the files of the "NAME CORRUPT" disk and to identify the name of the student whose files are now on this unusable disk.

INSTRUCTOR INFORMATION

WILD GOOSE MARINA, INC.

When To Use The *Wild Goose Marina Practice Set*

The **Wild Goose Marina** practice set is a computerized accounting simulation that offers students an opportunity to "practice" their accounting skills without spending hours preparing multiple statements, journals and ledgers. The set can be used with any **Principles of Accounting** text or **Intermediate Accounting** text. The **Wild Goose Marina** set can be used after the completion of the study of corporations, and stock and bond transactions of Principles texts or as a startup set for intensive review during the beginning weeks of an Intermediate Accounting class.

Hardware and Software Requirements

The minimum requirements for using the Wild Goose Marina software is an IBM PC or compatible with a minimum capacity of 640K and a DOS hosted operating system 2.0 or higher. If a problem occurs in booting the disk, check the system to be sure that other programs are not being automatically loaded into memory, thus reducing the memory available to operate the Wild Goose Marina system. (Wild Goose Marina has been successfully run on 512K systems.)

Software and Student Handbook Features

1. Full color and pull-down screens with easy to use menus

2. Pull-Down Screens
   A. Chart of Accounts (**F1 Key**)
   B. Vendor List (automatic)
   C. Customer List (automatic)

3. Automatic journalizing option using the pull down chart (**F1 Key**).

4. Automatic credit amount entry (**F10 Key**).

5. Automatic Closing Procedures
   A. Time-Saving, automatic closing entry procedure
   B. Follow-up questions on the closing entry process and results

6. Automatic Restoring--allows the student to restore balances to preclosing totals if corrections are necessary

7. Complete audit trail maintained through the journal and ledgers

8. Students are informed of each accounting procedure as it is performed by the computer system; for example: "Journal Entries Being Posted", "Subsidiary Ledger Being Posted", "General Ledger Being Closed", and others

9. Students can print or display a single general ledger account or subsidiary ledger account or print or display the entire subsidiary ledger for examination or analysis

10. Easier and faster data entry and an automatic "jump to" correction system

11. More check figures to enhance the student audit and error correction process

12. **Easy to use instructor reset disk that allows reset of a student disk to any week or to the beginning of the set**

13. Only two printing sessions required

14. Data entry can be made directly from source document to the computer

15. Two sets of evaluation questions with more intense coverage of the important accounting concepts--more efficient use of study time by the student and less paperwork to evaluate for the instructor

16. New protection system that eliminates any possibility of copying files from one disk to another

17. **Special instructor program included on the RESET Disk that can be used to determine if an attempt has been made to alter a student program disk**

Completion Time and Special Student Instructions

The average student will complete the **Wild Goose Marina, Inc.,** business simulation set in a ten to fourteen hours. Data entry, and printing time (computer time) will average from three to four hours. If the optional problems are included (four problems) in the assignment, up to three additional hours will be required to complete the set.

Extra reinforcement of these **key items** in the practice set may save your students considerable time and assist in maximizing their accounting experience.

1. The disk does require **special care and handling**.

2. Be sure to **Quit** after each journalizing session to transfer the data from the computer memory to the student disk.

3. Trial balances, all audit documents, and all required documents must be printed on an **as you go** basis. The account balances maintained are changed with each transaction. If a trial balance is printed for June 8, and then additional entries for the second week are entered, a correct trial balance for June 8 cannot be printed.

4. **PROPER ERROR CORRECTION PROCEDURES REQUIRE** that the error entry be completely **backed out** (reversed) and then the correct entry be recorded properly. This will leave a complete audit trail for the student and/or the instructor to follow. Detailed error correction procedure is introduced in the second entry of the set (June 1, page 17). A complete summary of the error correction process is found on pages 26 and 27 of the student manual.

What Students Need To Remember

To properly and efficiently operate the computerized accounting system used by Wild Goose Marina Inc., you must be familiar with several important computer procedures as well as business and account information details. These procedures and details are summarized in the list below and are introduced and explained in detail in the data entry procedures of the first week of your internship (June 1-8).

Typing **A:WILD** at the **C prompt** WILL NOT boot the disk! If using a computer with a hard disk, type **A:** at the **C prompt**. When the **A prompt** appears, type **WILD**.

The **F1** key may be used at **any account prompt** to display the **Chart of Accounts**. The chart of accounts may be used for faster data entry as well as for a quick reference to the number of each account in the chart of accounts.

The **F10** key will be used as a part of the "quick journal entry" process. After the debit/s have been entered, this key will automatically enter the amount of the credit entry (last credit entry if more than one credit).

A customer list with customer account numbers will automatically appear on the screen when the Accounts Receivable account is a part of the journal entry.

A vendor list with the vendor (creditor) account numbers will automatically appear on the screen when the Accounts Payable account is a part of the journal entry.

The **Esc** key may be used to exit quickly from all sub menus to the main menu. It may also be used in the **recording procedure to backup and erase an amount or an account**.

When entering transactions, always use proper accounting procedure and enter the debit entries **first**. When **debits** equal **credits** you will have a complete transaction to verify.

When several entries are to be entered on the same day, after the first journal entry has been entered and verified, press the **D** key at the date prompt to automatically enter the date for each additional transaction.

Error correction procedures for the Wild Goose Marina system require that the incorrect entry **be backed out (reversed) and then reentered correctly.** This correction procedure will be introduced in the first few transactions of the project. When an invoice number prompt, item prompt, or overhead prompt appears when entering a back out entry, enter **ERROR**. If an **error correction entry for cash** requires a credit to cash (and a check is not being issued), enter **ERROR** at the check number prompt. Additional detailed error correction instructions will be presented at the first check point (the end of the first week of transactions).

AT THE END OF EVERY JOURNALIZING SESSION, RETURN TO THE MAIN MENU. This procedure will post all of the transactions to the appropriate ledgers and transfer all data entered during the session from the computer memory to your disk.

You may terminate a journalizing session **at any time.** When you return to the journal entry process at a later time, the last entry recorded will be displayed on the screen.

At the end of each week, audit your work and make all of the necessary corrections required to match the "Check It Out" box. If printed documents are required, you must print the items **before continuing to the next week of transactions.** The system does not store end-of-week balances that can be printed later.

A May 31, 1997 Trial Balance, Schedule of Accounts Receivable, and **Schedule of Accounts Payable** are shown in the Appendix.

Making Copies or Backup Diskettes

1. **A PC with a hard disk drive and a single floppy disk drive.**

    Use the **DISKCOPY** command:

    C:>**DISKCOPY** [floppy disk drive]: [floppy disk drive]: and press the **Enter** key.

    Example: DISKCOPY A: A:

    Insert the source (original) disk and follow the instructions provided by DOS.

2. **A PC with two floppy drives (both 3.5" or both 5.25").**

    Place the source (original) disk in one drive and place a formatted (target) disk in the other disk drive.

    At the source disk-drive prompt type: **Copy*.*** [target disk drive]:***.*** and press the **Enter** key.

    Example: Copy*.* B:*.*

"Viruses"

It is recommended that the student disk be checked for viruses before:

   1. resetting the disk

   2. using the findname program

   3. checking the student disk for errors

Using the Reset Disk

The reset disk may be used at any time to reset a student disk or a replacement disk for a student to the end of any of the four data entry sessions. The reset may also be used to reset the student back to the beginning of the set, June 1, 1997.

When you have determined that it is appropriate to reset a student disk, complete the following:

1. Use a reset disk that is the same size as the student's disk (3.5" or 5.25").

2. Insert the reset disk in the disk drive and at the prompt for that drive type **RESET**.

3. When the Menu appears, select the appropriate week and press the **Enter** key.

4. When instructed, remove the reset disk and replace it with the student's disk. (3.5" or 5.25" Student Data Disk)

5. Press the **Enter** key and the disk will be reset.

You may continue to reset other disks or quit the reset program.

Using the FINDNAME Program

When a student reports a "NAME CORRUPT" error message, the name in the name file (name.) that is currently on the student disk is no longer the same as the name originally entered (initialized) on the student program disk.

These unmatched (corrupt) names will occur when a transfer is made of a name file from one program disk to another program disk that was *originally initialized by another user.*

Using **FINDNAME** will show the original user of the program disk.

1. Use a reset disk that is the same size as the student's disk (3.5" or 5.25").

2. Insert the reset disk in the disk drive and at the prompt type **FINDNAME** and press the **Enter** key.

3. At the first screen, press the **Enter** key.

4. When instructed, remove the reset disk and insert the student's disk in the disk drive.

5. Press the C key to continue.

6. The name originally entered on the source disk will now be shown on this program (target) disk.

    Example: Student Leland says his disk will not work because of a "NAME CORRUPT" error message. The FINDNAME program will show the source of the files now on Leland's disk. <u>*This disk cannot be reset!*</u>

7. Press any key to terminate the program.

Error Messages

The software contains routines to identify software and hardware errors. An error message will appear on the screen when the error is encountered. Some of the more common messages and their remedies are outlined below:

Error	Remedy
ERROR 7	*Computer is out of memory.* Perhaps the student's computer has Windows or other applications running in background, leaving insufficient memory to execute this simulation. The student may have to execute the program **directly** from DOS.
ERROR 9	Student has entered more journal entries than are required for this simulation, including a reasonable number of error corrections. Reset the student disk to the end of the week prior to the point of the numerous correcting entries.
Device Fault	Printer not turned on or not connected.
Out Of Paper	Replenish printer paper supply.
File Not Found	Review the instructions for accessing the proper disk drive (page 6 of the instructor manual, page 15 of the student manual). Check the disk for scratches, bends, other damage, or **viruses**.
Printer/Port Error	Printer not turned on or not connected or there is a serious hardware problem.
Disk Full	The student has made five or six times the number of corrections as there are total journal entries. Reset or replace the disk.
Disk Not Ready	Drive door open or no disk inserted. Check drive for disk and close the drive door.
Write Protected Disk	Write-protect tab on the diskette has been opened. Remove the disk, close the write-protect tab and reboot the program.
Disk Media Error	Sector/s on the disk have been damaged, replace the disk.

Loading the Program to a Hard Disk Drive

The program for this practice set is designed primarily for floppy disks. We do not encourage loading the program to a hard disk drive.

1. In a multiple computer laboratory, each student would need access to the computer on which the student's program had been copied.

2. Each student would need a separate directory on the hard disk for his/her program.

3. Students could exchange files between directories.

4. Resetting a student disk (correcting the student disk to the end of a particular week) would require transferring data files to the student directory from a floppy disk with the corrected data files transferred to it through the reset process. In other works, a backup disk (copy) would need to be reset to the end of the particular week, then the data files from this disk copied to the student directory on the hard drive.

Student's Personal Computer with a Hard Disk Drive

Should the student wish to use his/her own personal computer with a hard disk drive, provide the following information:

1. The student should establish a separate directory on the hard disk drive.

    C:>md C:\[directory name]

2. The student should copy only the 3.5" disk to the new directory.

    C:>Copy [A or B disk drive]:*.* C:\[new directory name]

NOTE: Resetting the student disk will require that the student be provided with a disk that is reset to the appropriate week to be recopied to the student's computer.

NOTE: Students should be encouraged to copy the directory of their disk to a formatted diskette at the end of each week as a "back up".

Black and White Monitors

With black and white monitors, some of the program menus may be difficult to read (they may appear as white on white). To overcome this, the user should use the DOS command titled **Mode**.

From DOS type:

      [disk drive]:>Mode BW80   or

      [disk drive]:>Mode Mono

      Example: A: Mode BW80

Faculty Service

Richard D. Irwin provides an Educational Software Services hotline to provide additional assistance for all instructors. The offices are located in Burr Ridge, Illinois and may be reached by calling **1-800 331-5094**.

STUDENT DOCUMENTS

For

JUNE 1-8

The student is not required to print any documents for June 1-8. These documents would be printed for audit purposes only.

STUDENT DOCUMENTS FOR JUNE 1-8

Wild Goose Marina, Incorporated
Trial Balance
June 8, 1997

	Accounts	Debit	Credit
101	Cash	$ 275,629.92	
102	Petty Cash	100.00	
103	Short-Term Investments	142,017.00	
105	Accounts Receivable	78,166.76	
106	Allowance for Doubtful Accounts		$ 1,867.00
109	Notes Receivable	212,050.00	
117	Merch. Inventory--Houseboats	315,200.00	
119	Merch. Inventory--Access.& Parts	41,132.00	
123	Prepaid Insurance	20,450.00	
124	Prepaid Rent	24,000.00	
129	Office Supplies	1,084.00	
131	Service & Shop Supplies	2,708.00	
140	Invest. in Baldwin Manufacturing	207,559.70	
141	Long-Term Investments	1,250,000.00	
145	Service & Shop Equipment	205,395.00	
146	Accum. Dep., Serv. & Shop Equip.		40,355.00
149	Trucks	48,550.00	
150	Accum. Depreciation, Trucks		28,250.00
153	Trailers	65,000.00	
154	Accum. Depreciation, Trailers		6,000.00
157	Office Equipment	12,960.00	
158	Accum. Deprec., Office Equip.		4,220.00
160	Leasehold	180,000.00	
165	Leasehold Improvements	325,000.00	
170	Patents	3,180.00	
175	Organization Costs	6,000.00	
201	Accounts Payable		31,674.00
203	Short-Term Notes Payable		90,000.00
211	Sales Tax Payable		28,950.38
215	Unearned Moorage Fees		72,550.00
225	State Unemployment Taxes Payable		278.14
227	Federal Unemployment Taxes Payable		92.71
235	Long-Term Lease Liability		6,500.00
236	Discount on Lease Financing	1,008.41	
241	Long-Term Notes Payable		115,000.00
242	Disc. on Long-Term Notes Pay.	8,125.00	

Continued on next page

STUDENT DOCUMENTS FOR JUNE 1-8

Continued from previous page

	Accounts	Debit	Credit
301	Preferred Stock		200,000.00
303	Contrib. Cap. in Exc. of Par, Pref.		20,000.00
305	Common Stock		2,300,000.00
308	Contrib. Cap. in Exc. of Par, Com.		78,500.00
315	Retained Earnings		110,724.86
320	Cash Dividends Declared	26,000.00	
401	Houseboat Sales		1,038,500.00
407	Accessories & Parts Sales		37,410.00
408	Access. & Parts Sales Ret. & Allow.	370.00	
412	Service Fees Earned		38,939.00
420	Sales Commissions Earned		15,100.00
501	Purchases--Houseboats	676,500.00	
502	Purchases Discounts--Houseboats		13,700.00
503	Transportation-In--Houseboats	13,105.00	
505	Purchases--Accessories & Parts	13,862.60	
506	Purch. Ret. & Allow.--Acc. & Parts		100.00
507	Purch. Discounts--Access. & Parts		497.45
508	Transportation-In--Access. & Parts	320.00	
601	Office & Shop Salaries & Wages Exp.	70,100.00	
602	Executive & Salespersons Salaries	36,000.00	
604	Equipment Rental Expense	4,500.00	
607	Truck Operating Expense	2,450.00	
608	Advertising Expense	2,119.75	
609	Credit Card Expense	196.21	
610	Delivery Expense	62.12	
611	Tools Expense	75.00	
619	Deprec. Expense, Office Equipment	400.00	
625	Electric & Gas Expense	1,312.00	
626	Telephone Expense	904.00	
627	Bank Service Charges	61.00	
628	Cash Short and Over	7.00	
629	License Expense	712.00	
630	Professional Services Expense	615.00	
631	Janitorial Services Expense	612.00	
635	Miscellaneous Expense	74.12	
711	Interest Earned		7,044.69
713	Dividends Earned		5,912.00
721	Gain on Sale of Assets		1,250.00
731	Gain on Short-Term Investments		200.00
741	Miscellaneous Revenue		56.00
813	Interest Expense	14,927.67	
821	Loss on Sale/Disposal of Assets	50.00	
825	Loss on Retirement of Bonds	1,679.97	
831	Loss on Short-Term Investments	135.00	
835	Loss on Long-Term Investments	1,205.00	
	Totals	$4,293,671.23	$4,293,671.23

STUDENT DOCUMENTS FOR JUNE 1-8

```
                         General Ledger Account
     CASH                                              Acct. No. 101
---------------------------------------------------------------------
  Date         Description         Debit       Credit       Balance
---------------------------------------------------------------------
June  1   Beginning Balance                                226,015.23
June  1   W2030                    106.92                  226,122.15
June  1   22334         03999                    19.75     226,102.40
June  1                             19.75                  226,122.15
June  1   22334         ERROR                    19.75     226,102.40
June  1   INTPA         04000                 6,000.00     220,102.40
June  2   BONDR         04001               206,000.00      14,102.40
June  3   W2031                 148,500.00                 162,602.40
June  3   PAYRL         04002                39,355.23     123,247.17
June  4   LRENT         04003                 1,500.00     121,747.17
June  4   W1995   11695          42,251.75                 163,998.92
June  5   W1901                  10,600.00                 174,598.92
June  5   DIVPA         04004                25,600.00     148,998.92
June  6   DISNT                 142,243.50                 291,242.42
June  7   K2244   22600  04005              254,800.00      36,442.42
June  8   SUBRE                 122,250.00                 158,692.42
June  8   FEDTX         04006                15,362.50     143,329.92
June  8   CSTOK                 128,500.00                 271,829.92
June  8   CASHD                   3,800.00                 275,629.92
=====================================================================
```

STUDENT DOCUMENTS FOR JUNE 1-8

General Journal Entries

June	1	Cash	101	106.92	
		Service Fees Earned	412		99.00
		Sales Tax Payable	211		7.92

           Invoice: W2030

June	1	Miscellaneous Expense	635	19.75	
		Cash	101		19.75

           Invoice: 22334
           Check: 03999

June	1	Cash	101	19.75	
		Miscellaneous Expense	635		19.75

June	1	Advertising Expense	608	19.75	
		Cash	101		19.75

           Invoice: 22334
           Check: ERROR

June	1	Office Supplies	129	108.00	
		Service & Shop Supplies	131	756.00	
		Accounts Payable	201		864.00

           Vendor: 24800
           Invoice: L2556

June	1	Purchases--Houseboats	501	10,500.00	
		Accounts Payable	201		10,500.00

           Vendor: 27125
           Invoice: S3344

June	1	Interest Payable	202	2,000.00	
		Premium on Bonds Payable	252	247.33	
		Interest Expense	813	3,752.67	
		Cash	101		6,000.00

           Invoice: INTPA
           Check: 04000

June	2	Bonds Payable	250	200,000.00	
		Premium on Bonds Payable	252	4,320.03	
		Loss on Retirement of Bonds	825	1,679.97	
		Cash	101		206,000.00

           Invoice: BONDR
           Check: 04001

STUDENT DOCUMENTS FOR JUNE 1-8

General Journal Entries

Date		Account	Acct #	Debit	Credit
June	3	Cash	101	148,500.00	
		Houseboat Sales	401		137,500.00
		Sales Tax Payable	211		11,000.00

Invoice: W2031

June	3	Salaries & Wages Payable	209	39,355.23	
		Cash	101		39,355.23

Invoice: PAYRL
Check: 04002

June	4	Accounts Receivable	105	1,346.76	
		Accessories & Parts Sales	407		522.00
		Service Fees Earned	412		725.00
		Sales Tax Payable	211		99.76

Customer: 10550
Invoice: W2032

June	4	Equipment Rental Expense	604	1,500.00	
		Cash	101		1,500.00

Invoice: LRENT
Check: 04003

June	4	Cash	101	42,251.75	
		Accounts Receivable	105		42,251.75

Customer: 11695
Invoice: W1995

June	4	Notes Receivable	109	6,500.00	
		Accounts Receivable	105		6,500.00

Customer: 11920
Invoice: NTREC

June	5	Cash	101	10,600.00	
		Notes Receivable	109		10,000.00
		Interest Earned	711		600.00

Invoice: W1901

June	5	Preferred Cash Dividends Payable	206	4,000.00	
		Common Cash Dividends Payable	208	21,600.00	
		Cash	101		25,600.00

Invoice: DIVPA
Check: 04004

STUDENT DOCUMENTS FOR JUNE 1-8

General Journal Entries

June	6	Service & Shop Equipment	145	16,875.00	
		Disc. on Long-Term Notes Pay.	242	8,125.00	
		Long-Term Notes Payable	241		25,000.00

    Invoice: X2990

June	6	Cash	101	142,243.50	
		Notes Receivable	109		140,000.00
		Interest Earned	711		2,243.50

    Invoice: DISNT

June	7	Accounts Payable	201	260,000.00	
		Cash	101		254,800.00
		Purchases Discounts--Houseboats	502		5,200.00

    Vendor: 22600
    Invoice: K2244
    Check: 04005

| June | 7 | Allowance for Doubtful Accounts | 106 | 550.00 | |
| | | Accounts Receivable | 105 | | 550.00 |

    Customer: 11350
    Invoice: WROFF

| June | 8 | Cash | 101 | 122,250.00 | |
| | | Subscriptions Rec., Common Stock | 116 | | 122,250.00 |

    Invoice: SUBRE

| June | 8 | Common Stock Subscribed | 306 | 200,000.00 | |
| | | Common Stock | 305 | | 200,000.00 |

    Invoice: SUBRE

June	8	Employee's Federal Inc. Taxes Pay.	221	7,355.00	
		FICA Taxes Payable	223	8,007.50	
		Cash	101		15,362.50

    Invoice: FEDTX
    Check: 04006

June	8	Cash	101	128,500.00	
		Common Stock	305		100,000.00
		Contrib. Cap. in Exc. of Par, Com.	308		28,500.00

    Invoice: CSTOK

| June | 8 | Cash | 101 | 3,800.00 | |
| | | Dividends Earned | 713 | | 3,800.00 |

    Invoice: CASHD

STUDENT DOCUMENTS

For

JUNE 9-15

The student is required to print all of the documents shown in this section except the General Journal.

STUDENT DOCUMENTS FOR JUNE 9-15

Wild Goose Marina, Incorporated
Trial Balance
June 15, 1997

	Accounts	Debit	Credit
101	Cash	$ 608,043.17	
102	Petty Cash	100.00	
103	Short-Term Investments	124,091.50	
105	Accounts Receivable	88,230.76	
106	Allowance for Doubtful Accounts		$ 2,299.00
109	Notes Receivable	212,050.00	
117	Merch. Inventory--Houseboats	315,200.00	
119	Merch. Inventory--Access.& Parts	41,132.00	
123	Prepaid Insurance	20,450.00	
124	Prepaid Rent	24,000.00	
129	Office Supplies	1,621.97	
131	Service & Shop Supplies	2,708.00	
140	Invest. in Baldwin Manufacturing	207,559.70	
141	Long-Term Investments	1,250,000.00	
145	Service & Shop Equipment	205,395.00	
146	Accum. Dep., Serv. & Shop Equip.		40,355.00
149	Trucks	42,600.00	
150	Accum. Depreciation, Trucks		12,950.00
153	Trailers	65,000.00	
154	Accum. Depreciation, Trailers		6,000.00
157	Office Equipment	12,010.00	
158	Accum. Deprec., Office Equip.		3,395.00
160	Leasehold	180,000.00	
165	Leasehold Improvements	325,000.00	
170	Patents	3,180.00	
175	Organization Costs	6,000.00	
201	Accounts Payable		17,697.97
203	Short-Term Notes Payable		90,000.00
211	Sales Tax Payable		29,862.38
215	Unearned Moorage Fees		82,725.00
225	State Unemployment Taxes Payable		278.14
227	Federal Unemployment Taxes Payable		92.71
235	Long-Term Lease Liability		6,500.00
236	Discount on Lease Financing	1,008.41	
241	Long-Term Notes Payable		115,000.00
242	Disc. on Long-Term Notes Pay.	8,125.00	
250	Bonds Payable		400,000.00
251	Discount on Bonds Payable	16,340.20	

Continued on next page

STUDENT DOCUMENTS FOR JUNE 9-15

Continued from previous page

	Accounts	Debit	Credit
301	Preferred Stock		200,000.00
303	Contrib. Cap. in Exc. of Par, Pref.		20,000.00
305	Common Stock		2,300,000.00
307	Common Stock Dividend Distrib.		23,000.00
308	Contrib. Cap. in Exc. of Par, Com.		85,515.00
315	Retained Earnings		110,724.86
320	Cash Dividends Declared	26,000.00	
325	Stock Dividends Declared	30,015.00	
330	Treasury Stock	40,575.00	
401	Houseboat Sales		1,038,500.00
407	Accessories & Parts Sales		41,310.00
408	Access. & Parts Sales Ret. & Allow.	370.00	
412	Service Fees Earned		46,439.00
420	Sales Commissions Earned		18,070.00
501	Purchases--Houseboats	676,500.00	
502	Purchases Discounts--Houseboats		13,700.00
503	Transportation-In--Houseboats	13,105.00	
505	Purchases--Accessories & Parts	13,862.60	
506	Purch. Ret. & Allow.--Acc. & Parts		100.00
507	Purch. Discounts--Access. & Parts		633.95
508	Transportation-In--Access. & Parts	320.00	
601	Office & Shop Salaries & Wages Exp.	70,100.00	
602	Executive & Salespersons Salaries	36,000.00	
604	Equipment Rental Expense	4,500.00	
607	Truck Operating Expense	2,450.00	
608	Advertising Expense	2,743.75	
609	Credit Card Expense	196.21	
610	Delivery Expense	79.67	
611	Tools Expense	75.00	
619	Deprec. Expense, Office Equipment	450.00	
625	Electric & Gas Expense	1,312.00	
626	Telephone Expense	904.00	
627	Bank Service Charges	61.00	
628	Cash Short and Over	7.00	
629	License Expense	712.00	
630	Professional Services Expense	615.00	
631	Janitorial Services Expense	612.00	
635	Miscellaneous Expense	74.12	
711	Interest Earned		7,044.69
713	Dividends Earned		6,432.00
721	Gain on Sale of Assets		1,525.00
731	Gain on Short-Term Investments		10,957.00
741	Miscellaneous Revenue		76.00
811	Income Taxes Expense	31,500.00	
813	Interest Expense	14,927.67	
821	Loss on Sale/Disposal of Assets	250.00	
825	Loss on Retirement of Bonds	1,679.97	
831	Loss on Short-Term Investments	135.00	
835	Loss on Long-Term Investments	1,205.00	
	Totals	$4,731,182.70	$4,731,182.70

STUDENT DOCUMENTS FOR JUNE 9-15

Wild Goose Marina, Incorporated
Schedule of Accounts Receivable
June 15, 1997

Customer Number	Customer Name	Account Balance
10200	Adams Farms Incorporated	$ 15,000.00
10550	Bettencourt, Inc.	58,346.76
10820	R. J. Corsetti	1,988.00
11050	J. P. Elam	4,016.00
11185	Joan Kuhlman	0.00
11260	Kingston & Sons, Inc.	6,210.00
11350	Dale Novice	0.00
11405	Randy Robberts	0.00
11470	Roseburg & Associates	0.00
11520	Taylor Company	2,670.00
11695	Tisedaile Const. Co.	0.00
11920	Zakk, Incorporated	0.00
Totals		$ 88,230.76

STUDENT DOCUMENTS FOR JUNE 9-15

Accounts Receivable Subsidiary Ledger

Page 1

Adams Farms Incorporated
3354 East Avenue
Placerville, CA

No. 10200

Date	Description		Debit	Credit	Balance
May 25	W2015		15,000.00		15,000.00

Bettencourt, Inc.
8000 Baywood Street
Sacramento, CA

No. 10550

Date	Description		Debit	Credit	Balance
May 28	W2024		57,000.00		57,000.00
June 4	W2032		1,346.76		58,346.76

R. J. Corsetti
6677 Hill Road
Auburn, CA

No. 10820

Date	Description		Debit	Credit	Balance
May 17	W1995		2,150.00		2,150.00
June 14	CM201	W1995		162.00	1,988.00

J. P. Elam
6525 Carolinda Dr.
Forest Hill, CA

No. 11050

Date	Description		Debit	Credit	Balance
Jan. 1	W1760		432.00		432.00
Apr. 20	W1760	WROFF		432.00	0.00
June 9	RECOV		432.00		432.00
June 9		RECOV		432.00	0.00
June 14	BADCK		4,016.00		4,016.00

Continued next page...

STUDENT DOCUMENTS FOR JUNE 9-15

Accounts Receivable Subsidiary Ledger   Page   2

Joan Kuhlman
4588 Gold Run Road
Malibu, CA   No. 11185

   Date   Description   Debit   Credit   Balance

   June 1   Beginning Balance   0.00

Kingston & Sons, Inc.
456 Snowcrest Court
Fair Oaks, CA   No. 11260

   Date   Description   Debit   Credit   Balance

   June 1   Beginning Balance   0.00
   June 9   W2033   6,210.00   6,210.00

Dale Novice
5550 Rock Road
Oakland, CA   No. 11350

   Date   Description   Debit   Credit   Balance

   Feb. 1   W1805   550.00   550.00
   June 7   WROFF   550.00   0.00

Randy Robberts
456 GEO Drive
Grass Valley, CA   No. 11405

   Date   Description   Debit   Credit   Balance

   June 1   Beginning Balance   0.00

Roseburg & Associates
444 3rd Ave. Suite B
Yuba City, CA   No. 11470

   Date   Description   Debit   Credit   Balance

   June 1   Beginning Balance   0.00

Continued next page...

STUDENT DOCUMENTS FOR JUNE 9-15

Accounts Receivable Subsidiary Ledger   Page 3

Taylor Company
5162 Brook Court
Clayton, CA   No. 11520

Date	Description	Debit	Credit	Balance
Jan. 1	W1761	2,670.00		2,670.00

Tisedaile Const. Co.
123 Ball Court
Hoop, OR   No. 11695

Date	Description	Debit	Credit	Balance
May 4	W1955	42,251.75		42,251.75
June 4	W1995		42,251.75	0.00

Zakk, Incorporated
1313 Pine Drive
Granite Bay, CA   No. 11920

Date	Description	Debit	Credit	Balance
May 1	W1950	6,500.00		6,500.00
June 4	NTREC		6,500.00	0.00

STUDENT DOCUMENTS FOR JUNE 9-15

Wild Goose Marina, Incorporated
Schedule of Accounts Payable
June 15, 1997

Vendor Number	Vendor Name		Account Balance
20500	Corr Marine Supply	$	0.00
21990	Foster Business Supply		6,660.00
22600	Kruzer Houseboats		0.00
24800	Luzzi, Incorporated		0.00
25950	Quinlivin, Incorporated		0.00
26675	Reading Real Estate		0.00
27005	Rockwood Business Supply		537.97
27125	Snow Goose Houseboats		10,500.00
28400	Yee & Associates, Inc.		0.00
Totals		$	17,697.97

STUDENT DOCUMENTS FOR JUNE 9-15

Accounts Payable Subsidiary Ledger

Page 1

Corr Marine Supply
4455 Stone Court
  Loomis, CA   1/15, n/30   No. 20500

Date	Description	Debit	Credit	Balance
May 26	C6211		13,650.00	13,650.00
June 11	C6211 04008	13,650.00		0.00

Foster Business Supply
5114 Santa Clara
  Anderson, CA   2/10, n/30   No. 21990

Date	Description	Debit	Credit	Balance
May 29	F1466		6,660.00	6,660.00

Kruzer Houseboats
6666 Pontoon Way
  Redding, CA   2/10, n/30   No. 22600

Date	Description	Debit	Credit	Balance
May 28	K2244		260,000.00	260,000.00
June 7	K2244 04005	260,000.00		0.00

Luzzi, Incorporated
690 Fairhaven Court
  Rio Linda, CA Net 10   No. 24800

Date	Description	Debit	Credit	Balance
Beginning Balance				0.00
June 1	L2556		864.00	864.00
June 12	L2256 04009	864.00		0.00

Quinlivin, Incorporated
5555 Firecrst Road
  Colfax, Ca   Net 30   No. 25950

Date	Description	Debit	Credit	Balance
Beginning Balance				0.00

Continued next page...

STUDENT DOCUMENTS FOR JUNE 9-15

Accounts Payable Subsidiary Ledger   Page   2

Reading Real Estate
4005 Magnolia Ave.
  Sacramento, CA 2/10, n/30   No. 26675

  Date   Description   Debit   Credit   Balance

Beginning Balance   0.00

Rockwood Business Supply
2105 Baylor Road
  Auburn, CA   Net 30   No. 27005

  Date   Description   Debit   Credit   Balance

Beginning Balance   0.00
  June 13   55663   566.22   566.22
  June 14   55663   28.25   537.97

Snow Goose Houseboats
111 Cackler Circle
  Honker Bay, WA Net 30   No. 27125

  Date   Description   Debit   Credit   Balance

Beginning Balance   0.00
  June 2   S3344   10,500.00   10,500.00

Yee & Associates, Inc.
4436 Bayye Street
  Rocklin, CA   Net 30   No. 28400

  Date   Description   Debit   Credit   Balance

Beginning Balance   0.00

STUDENT DOCUMENTS FOR JUNE 9-15

```
                          General Ledger Account
     CASH                                                  Acct. No. 101
------------------------------------------------------------------------
    Date           Description            Debit         Credit     Balance
------------------------------------------------------------------------
    June  1    Beginning Balance                                  226,015.23
    June  1    W2030                      106.92                  226,122.15
    June  1    22334         03999                        19.75   226,102.40
    June  1                                19.75                  226,122.15
    June  1    22334         ERROR                        19.75   226,102.40
    June  1    INTPA         04000                     6,000.00   220,102.40
    June  2    BONDR         04001                   206,000.00    14,102.40
    June  3    W2031                  148,500.00                  162,602.40
    June  3    PAYRL         04002                    39,355.23   123,247.17
    June  4    LRENT         04003                     1,500.00   121,747.17
    June  4    W1995  11695              42,251.75                163,998.92
    June  5    W1901                   10,600.00                  174,598.92
    June  5    DIVPA         04004                    25,600.00   148,998.92
    June  6    DISNT                  142,243.50                  291,242.42
    June  7    K2244  22600  04005                   254,800.00    36,442.42
    June  8    SUBRE                  122,250.00                  158,692.42
    June  8    FEDTX         04006                    15,362.50   143,329.92
    June  8    CSTOK                  128,500.00                  271,829.92
    June  8    CASHD                    3,800.00                  275,629.92
    June  9    RECOV  11050              432.00                   276,061.92
    June  9    CE601                    2,970.00                  279,031.92
    June  9    STOKS                   28,682.50                  307,714.42
    June 10    ASALE                      350.00                  308,064.42
    June 10    HF244         04007                       624.00   307,440.42
    June 11    C6211  20500  04008                    13,513.50   293,926.92
    June 11    L2256  24800  04009                       864.00   293,062.92
    June 12    TSTOK         04010                    40,575.00   252,487.92
    June 13    W2034                    2,268.00                  254,755.92
    June 13    W2035                    3,996.00                  258,751.92
    June 13    CASHD                      520.00                  259,271.92
    June 14    W2030  11050  BADCK                     3,996.00   255,275.92
    June 15    Q1521         04011                        17.55   255,258.37
    June 15    EXTRA         04012                     9,550.00   245,708.37
    June 15    BONDS                  383,659.80                  629,368.17
    June 15    MF061                   10,175.00                  639,543.17
    June 15    INCTX         04013                    31,500.00   608,043.17
========================================================================
```

STUDENT DOCUMENTS FOR JUNE 9-15

General Ledger Account
ACCOUNTS RECEIVABLE   Acct. No. 105

Date	Description			Debit	Credit	Balance
June 1	Beginning Balance					126,121.75
June 4	W2032	10550		1,346.76		127,468.51
June 4	W1995	11695			42,251.75	85,216.76
June 4	NTREC	11920			6,500.00	78,716.76
June 7	WROFF	11350			550.00	78,166.76
June 9	RECOV	11050		432.00		78,598.76
June 9	RECOV	11050			432.00	78,166.76
June 9	W2033	11260		6,210.00		84,376.76
June 14	W1995	10820	CM201		162.00	84,214.76
June 14	W2030	11050	BADCK	4,016.00		88,230.76

===

General Ledger Account
ALLOWANCE FOR DOUBTFUL ACCOUNTS   Acct. No. 106

Date	Description		Debit	Credit	Balance
June 1	Beginning Balance				2,417.00
June 7	WROFF	11350	550.00		1,867.00
June 9	RECOV	11050		432.00	2,299.00

===

General Ledger Account
ACCOUNTS PAYABLE   Acct. No. 201

Date	Description			Debit	Credit	Balance
June 1	Beginning Balance					280,310.00
June 1	L2556	24800			864.00	281,174.00
June 1	S3344	27125			10,500.00	291,674.00
June 7	K2244	22600	04005	260,000.00		31,674.00
June 11	C6211	20500	04008	13,650.00		18,024.00
June 11	L2256	24800	04009	864.00		17,160.00
June 13	55663	27005			566.22	17,726.22
June 14	55663	27005		28.25		17,697.97

===

STUDENT DOCUMENTS FOR JUNE 9-15

General Ledger Account
TREASURY STOCK — Acct. No. 330

Date	Description	Debit	Credit	Balance
June 1	Beginning Balance			0.00
June 12	TSTOK 04010	40,575.00		40,575.00

General Ledger Account
SERVICE FEES EARNED — Acct. No. 412

Date	Description	Debit	Credit	Balance
June 1	Beginning Balance			38,115.00
June 1	W2030		99.00	38,214.00
June 4	W2032 10550		725.00	38,939.00
June 9	W2033 11260		5,100.00	44,039.00
June 13	W2034		2,100.00	46,139.00
June 13	W2035		450.00	46,589.00
June 14	W1995 10820 CM201	150.00		46,439.00

General Ledger Account
DIVIDENDS EARNED — Acct. No. 713

Date	Description	Debit	Credit	Balance
June 1	Beginning Balance			2,112.00
June 8	CASHD		3,800.00	5,912.00
June 13	CASHD		520.00	6,432.00

STUDENT DOCUMENTS FOR JUNE 9-15

General Journal Entries

Date		Account	Acct#	Debit	Credit
June	9	Accounts Receivable	105	432.00	
		Allowance for Doubtful Accounts	106		432.00

      Customer: 11050
      Invoice: RECOV

June	9	Cash	101	432.00	
		Accounts Receivable	105		432.00

      Customer: 11050
      Invoice: RECOV

June	9	Cash	101	2,970.00	
		Sales Commissions Earned	420		2,970.00

      Invoice: CE601

June	9	Cash	101	28,682.50	
		Short-Term Investments	103		17,925.50
		Gain on Short-Term Investments	731		10,757.00

      Invoice: STOKS

June	9	Accounts Receivable	105	6,210.00	
		Accessories & Parts Sales	407		650.00
		Service Fees Earned	412		5,100.00
		Sales Tax Payable	211		460.00

      Customer: 11260
      Invoice: W2033

June	9	Accum. Depreciation, Trucks	150	5,750.00	
		Loss on Sale/Disposal of Assets	821	200.00	
		Trucks	149		5,950.00

      Invoice: DONAT

June	10	Deprec. Expense, Office Equipment	619	50.00	
		Accum. Deprec., Office Equip.	158		50.00

June	10	Cash	101	350.00	
		Accum. Deprec., Office Equip.	158	875.00	
		Office Equipment	157		950.00
		Gain on Sale of Assets	721		275.00

      Invoice: ASALE

STUDENT DOCUMENTS FOR JUNE 9-15

General Journal Entries

Date	Account	Acct#	Debit	Credit
June 10	Advertising Expense	608	624.00	
	Cash	101		624.00
	Invoice: HF244			
	Check: 04007			
June 10	Accounts Payable	201	13,650.00	
	Cash	101		13,513.50
	Purch. Discounts--Access. & Parts	507		136.50
	Vendor: 20500			
	Invoice: C6211			
	Check: 04008			
June 11	Stock Dividends Declared	325	30,015.00	
	Common Stock Dividend Distrib.	307		23,000.00
	Contrib. Cap. in Exc. of Par, Com.	308		7,015.00
	Invoice: STKDV			
June 11	Accounts Payable	201	864.00	
	Cash	101		864.00
	Vendor: 24800			
	Invoice: L2256			
	Check: 04009			
June 12	Treasury Stock	330	40,575.00	
	Cash	101		40,575.00
	Invoice: TSTOK			
	Check: 04010			
June 13	Cash	101	2,268.00	
	Service Fees Earned	412		2,100.00
	Sales Tax Payable	211		168.00
	Invoice: W2034			
June 13	Cash	101	3,996.00	
	Accessories & Parts Sales	407		3,250.00
	Service Fees Earned	412		450.00
	Sales Tax Payable	211		296.00
	Invoice: W2035			

STUDENT DOCUMENTS FOR JUNE 9-15

General Journal Entries

Date	Account	Acct #	Debit	Credit
June 13	Office Supplies	129	566.22	
	Accounts Payable	201		566.22
	Vendor: 27005			
	Invoice: 55663			
June 13	Cash	101	520.00	
	Dividends Earned	713		520.00
	Invoice: CASHD			
June 14	Accounts Payable	201	28.25	
	Office Supplies	129		28.25
	Vendor: 27005			
	Invoice: 55663			
June 14	Service Fees Earned	412	150.00	
	Sales Tax Payable	211	12.00	
	Accounts Receivable	105		162.00
	Customer: 10820			
	Invoice: W1995			
	Credit Memo: CM201			
June 14	Accounts Receivable	105	4,016.00	
	Cash	101		3,996.00
	Miscellaneous Revenue	741		20.00
	Customer: 11050			
	Invoice: W2030			
	Check: BADCK			
June 15	Delivery Expense	610	17.55	
	Cash	101		17.55
	Invoice: Q1521			
	Check: 04011			
June 15	Accum. Depreciation, Trucks	150	9,550.00	
	Cash	101		9,550.00
	Invoice: EXTRA			
	Check: 04012			
June 15	Cash	101	383,659.80	
	Discount on Bonds Payable	251	16,340.20	
	Bonds Payable	250		400,000.00
	Invoice: BONDS			

STUDENT DOCUMENTS FOR JUNE 9-15

General Journal Entries

June 15	Cash		101	10,175.00	
		Unearned Moorage Fees	215		10,175.00
	Invoice: MF061				
June 15	Income Taxes Expense		811	31,500.00	
		Cash	101		31,500.00
	Invoice: INCAX				
	Check: 04013				

MID-PROJECT EVALUATION

WILD GOOSE MARINA, INC.

June 15, 1997

MID-PROJECT EVALUATION   NAME_____

WILD GOOSE MARINA, INCORPORATED   SECTION_____ DATE_____

1. Do the balances on your printed Trial Balance match the amounts shown in the "Check It Out" block?

    YES   X   NO_____

2. What was the *correct* balance of the Cash account at the close of business on June 9?

    $ 307,714.42

3. What invoice was paid in full with check number 04005 on June 7?

    Invoice Number   K2244

4. What was the correct balance of the Accounts Receivable account after the first accounts receivable entry of June 4?

    $ 127,468.51

5-6. An entry for $6,210.00 was debited to the Accounts Receivable account on June 9. Which customer was involved in this transaction (identify by number) and what was the sales invoice number?

    Customer Number 11260

    Invoice Number W2033

7. An entry for $6,500.00 was credited to the Accounts Receivable account on June 4. What was the reason for this credit?

    Exchange for a Note Receivable

8. At the close of business on June 13, what was the balance of the Accounts Payable account?

    $ 17,726.22

9-10. On June 11, an entry for $13,650.00 was debited to the Accounts Payable account. Identify the name of the vendor/creditor and the number of the invoice paid.

    Vendor/Creditor Name   Corr Marine Supply

    Invoice Number   C6211

11. When the Treasury Stock account has a normal balance does it *increase* or *decrease* the value of the stockholders' equity?

    Decrease

12. How much was earned in Service Fees on June 13?

    $ 2,550.00

13. Why was the Service Fees account debited on June 14?

    Corrected the Overcharge

14. What is the total amount of dividends earned that had been reported as of the close of business June 8?

    $ 5,912.00

15. On June 15, which customer has the largest outstanding balance?

    Customer Number 10550

MID-PROJECT EVALUATION
WILD GOOSE MARINA, INCORPORATED

16. Explain the activity in the J. P. Elam account on June 9. — **Bad Debt Recovery**

17-18. Which customer was issued credit memo CM201 and what was the account balance after the credit to the customer's account? — **Customer Number 10820** / **$ 1,988.00**

19. Customer accounts are due 30 days after the invoice date. Carefully examine the Accounts Receivable subsidiary ledger. Identify by name the customer whose account is past due. — **Customer Name Taylor Company**

20. Why does the Dale Novice account now have a $0.00 balance? — **The Account Was Written Off**

21. Before the June 4 entry, what was the balance of the Tisedaile Construction Company account? — **$ 42,251.75**

22. Does the balance of the Schedule of Accounts Receivable match the balance of the Accounts Receivable account? — **YES   X   NO**

23. If financial statements were prepared as of June 15, what would be the reported Net Accounts Receivable balance? — **$ 85,931.76**

24. What terms are extended by the Corr Marine Supply? — **1/15, n/30**

25. What was the balance of the Corr Marine Supply accounts payable account before payment of June 11? — **$ 13,650.00**

26-27. Due to a filing error, one account in the Accounts Payable subsidiary ledger is past the discount period. Identify the account and calculate the amount of the discount that has been lost due to this oversight. — **Vendor Number 21990** / **$ 133.20**

28. What amount of cash was required to pay off the Kruzer Houseboats account balance on June 7? — **$ 254,800.00**

29. Explain the reason for the $28.25 reduction in the balance owed to Rockwood Business Supply. — **Return of Supplies**

30. On what date is the balance owed to Rockwood Business Supply due and payable? — **Date July 13**

31. What has been the net amount of increase in all forms of long-term debt since the May 31 Trial Balance? — **$ 195,967.47**

32. What is the total amount of contributed capital on June 15? — **$ 2,628,515.00**

MID-PROJECT EVALUATION
WILD GOOSE MARINA, INCORPORATED

33. Net Accessories & Parts Sales are what percent of total <u>Net Sales</u> as of June 15?   <u>**3.79%**</u>

34-35. What has been the total increase or decrease in the carrying value (net liability) of bonds payable since the May 31 Trial Balance?   <u>**$ 179,092.44**</u>

<u>**Increase**</u>

STUDENT DOCUMENTS

For

JUNE 16-22

The student is not required to print any documents for June 16-22. These documents would be printed for audit purposes only.

STUDENT DOCUMENTS FOR JUNE 16-22

Wild Goose Marina, Incorporated
Trial Balance
June 22, 1997

	Accounts	Debit	Credit
101	Cash	$ 564,134.97	
102	Petty Cash	100.00	
103	Short-Term Investments	124,091.50	
105	Accounts Receivable	197,029.76	
106	Allowance for Doubtful Accounts		$ 204.00
109	Notes Receivable	212,050.00	
116	Subscriptions Rec., Common Stock	92,400.00	
117	Merch. Inventory--Houseboats	315,200.00	
119	Merch. Inventory--Access.& Parts	41,132.00	
123	Prepaid Insurance	21,650.00	
124	Prepaid Rent	24,000.00	
129	Office Supplies	1,621.97	
131	Service & Shop Supplies	2,708.00	
140	Invest. in Baldwin Manufacturing	224,509.70	
141	Long-Term Investments	1,255,955.50	
145	Service & Shop Equipment	196,795.00	
146	Accum. Dep., Serv. & Shop Equip.		32,855.00
149	Trucks	62,850.00	
150	Accum. Depreciation, Trucks		3,950.00
153	Trailers	65,000.00	
154	Accum. Depreciation, Trailers		6,000.00
157	Office Equipment	12,010.00	
158	Accum. Deprec., Office Equip.		3,395.00
160	Leasehold	180,000.00	
165	Leasehold Improvements	400,000.00	
170	Patents	3,180.00	
175	Organization Costs	6,000.00	
201	Accounts Payable		453,802.66
211	Sales Tax Payable		18,216.66
215	Unearned Moorage Fees		82,725.00
225	State Unemployment Taxes Payable		278.14
227	Federal Unemployment Taxes Payable		92.71
235	Long-Term Lease Liability		6,500.00
236	Discount on Lease Financing	1,008.41	
241	Long-Term Notes Payable		115,000.00
242	Disc. on Long-Term Notes Pay.	8,125.00	
250	Bonds Payable		400,000.00
251	Discount on Bonds Payable	16,340.20	

Continued on next page

STUDENT DOCUMENTS FOR JUNE 16-22

Continued from previous page

	Accounts	Debit	Credit
301	Preferred Stock		200,000.00
303	Contrib. Cap. in Exc. of Par, Pref.		20,000.00
305	Common Stock		2,300,000.00
306	Common Stock Subscribed		100,000.00
307	Common Stock Dividend Distrib.		23,000.00
308	Contrib. Cap. in Exc. of Par, Com.		117,515.00
315	Retained Earnings		110,024.86
320	Cash Dividends Declared	26,000.00	
325	Stock Dividends Declared	30,015.00	
330	Treasury Stock	27,050.00	
401	Houseboat Sales		1,253,777.78
407	Accessories & Parts Sales		41,310.00
408	Access. & Parts Sales Ret. & Allow.	370.00	
412	Service Fees Earned		58,869.56
420	Sales Commissions Earned		18,070.00
501	Purchases--Houseboats	1,086,000.00	
502	Purchases Discounts--Houseboats		13,700.00
503	Transportation-In--Houseboats	31,605.00	
505	Purchases--Accessories & Parts	21,967.29	
506	Purch. Ret. & Allow.--Acc. & Parts		100.00
507	Purch. Discounts--Access. & Parts		633.95
508	Transportation-In--Access. & Parts	320.00	
601	Office & Shop Salaries & Wages Exp.	70,100.00	
602	Executive & Salespersons Salaries	36,000.00	
604	Equipment Rental Expense	4,500.00	
607	Truck Operating Expense	2,450.00	
608	Advertising Expense	2,743.75	
609	Credit Card Expense	196.21	
610	Delivery Expense	79.67	
611	Tools Expense	146.32	
613	Deprec. Exp., Serv. & Shop Equip.	300.00	
615	Deprec. Expense, Trucks	750.00	
619	Deprec. Expense, Office Equipment	450.00	
625	Electric & Gas Expense	1,312.00	
626	Telephone Expense	904.00	
627	Bank Service Charges	61.00	
628	Cash Short and Over	7.00	
629	License Expense	1,407.50	
630	Professional Services Expense	1,440.00	
631	Janitorial Services Expense	966.50	
635	Miscellaneous Expense	74.12	
711	Interest Earned		7,044.69
713	Dividends Earned		6,432.00
715	Earnings on Investments		16,950.00
721	Gain on Sale of Assets		3,325.00
731	Gain on Short-Term Investments		10,957.00
741	Miscellaneous Revenue		76.00
811	Income Taxes Expense	31,500.00	
813	Interest Expense	14,927.67	
821	Loss on Sale/Disposal of Assets	250.00	
825	Loss on Retirement of Bonds	1,679.97	
831	Loss on Short-Term Investments	135.00	
835	Loss on Long-Term Investments	1,205.00	
	Totals	$5,424,805.01	$5,424,805.01

STUDENT DOCUMENTS FOR JUNE 16-22

General Journal Entries

June 16	Long-Term Investments	141	5,955.50	
	Cash	101		5,955.50
	Invoice: INVST			
	Check: 04014			
June 16	Accounts Receivable	105	102,060.00	
	Cash	101		102,060.00
	Customer: 11405			
	Invoice: W1855			
	Check: DISHO			
June 17	Cash	101	12,825.00	
	Retained Earnings	315	700.00	
	Treasury Stock	330		13,525.00
	Invoice: TSTOK			
June 17	Sales Tax Payable	211	29,862.38	
	Cash	101		29,862.38
	Invoice: SALTX			
	Check: 04015			
June 17	Purchases--Houseboats	501	409,500.00	
	Transportation-In--Houseboats	503	18,500.00	
	Accounts Payable	201		428,000.00
	Vendor: 22600			
	Invoice: K3556			
June 17	Deprec. Exp., Serv. & Shop Equip.	613	300.00	
	Accum. Dep., Serv. & Shop Equip.	146		300.00
June 17	Cash	101	2,600.00	
	Accum. Dep., Serv. & Shop Equip.	146	7,800.00	
	Service & Shop Equipment	145		8,600.00
	Gain on Sale of Assets	721		1,800.00
	Invoice: ASALE			
June 18	Cash	101	4,016.00	
	Accounts Receivable	105		4,016.00
	Customer: 11050			
	Invoice: W2035			

STUDENT DOCUMENTS FOR JUNE 16-22

General Journal Entries

Date	Account	Acct#	Debit	Credit
June 18	Janitorial Services Expense	631	354.50	
	Cash	101		354.50
	Invoice: 12655			
	Check: 04016			
June 18	Professional Services Expense	630	825.00	
	Cash	101		825.00
	Invoice: SS301			
	Check: 04017			
June 19	Cash	101	575.00	
	Allowance for Doubtful Accounts	106	2,095.00	
	Accounts Receivable	105		2,670.00
	Customer: 11520			
	Invoice: WROFF			
June 19	Subscriptions Rec., Common Stock	116	132,000.00	
	Common Stock Subscribed	306		100,000.00
	Contrib. Cap. in Exc. of Par, Com.	308		32,000.00
	Invoice: SUBRE			
June 19	Cash	101	39,600.00	
	Subscriptions Rec., Common Stock	116		39,600.00
	Invoice: SUBRE			
June 19	Prepaid Insurance	123	1,200.00	
	Cash	101		1,200.00
	Invoice: DP651			
	Check: 04018			
June 19	Short-Term Notes Payable	203	90,000.00	
	Cash	101		90,000.00
	Invoice: DISNT			
	Check: 04019			
June 20	Tools Expense	611	71.32	
	Cash	101		71.32
	Invoice: 11334			
	Check: 04020			

STUDENT DOCUMENTS FOR JUNE 16-22

General Journal Entries

Date	Account	Ref	Debit	Credit
June 20	Purchases--Accessories & Parts	505	8,104.69	
	Accounts Payable	201		8,104.69
	Vendor: 28400			
	Invoice: T3555			
June 21	Cash	101	232,500.00	
	Houseboat Sales	401		215,277.78
	Sales Tax Payable	211		17,222.22
	Invoice: W2036			
June 21	Invest. in Baldwin Manufacturing	140	16,950.00	
	Earnings on Investments	715		16,950.00
	Invoice: EARNS			
June 22	Accounts Receivable	105	13,425.00	
	Service Fees Earned	412		12,430.56
	Sales Tax Payable	211		994.44
	Customer: 11470			
	Invoice: W2037			
June 22	Deprec. Expense, Trucks	615	750.00	
	Accum. Depreciation, Trucks	150		750.00
June 22	Trucks	149	32,850.00	
	Accum. Depreciation, Trucks	150	9,750.00	
	Cash	101		30,000.00
	Trucks	149		12,600.00
	Invoice: N1566			
	Check: 04021			
June 22	License Expense	629	695.50	
	Cash	101		695.50
	Invoice: DMV06			
	Check: 04022			
June 22	Leasehold Improvements	165	75,000.00	
	Cash	101		75,000.00
	Invoice: G7777			
	Check: 04023			

STUDENT DOCUMENTS

For

JUNE 23-30

The student is not required to print any documents for June 23-30. These documents would be printed for audit purposes only.

STUDENT DOCUMENTS FOR JUNE 23-30

Wild Goose Marina, Incorporated
Trial Balance
June 30, 1997

	Accounts	Debit	Credit
101	Cash	$ 174,707.65	
102	Petty Cash	100.00	
103	Short-Term Investments	119,999.50	
105	Accounts Receivable	79,969.76	
106	Allowance for Doubtful Accounts		$ 204.00
109	Notes Receivable	221,500.00	
116	Subscriptions Rec., Common Stock	92,400.00	
117	Merch. Inventory--Houseboats	315,200.00	
119	Merch. Inventory--Access.& Parts	41,132.00	
123	Prepaid Insurance	21,650.00	
124	Prepaid Rent	24,000.00	
129	Office Supplies	1,632.47	
131	Service & Shop Supplies	2,854.88	
140	Invest. in Baldwin Manufacturing	218,509.70	
141	Long-Term Investments	1,255,955.50	
145	Service & Shop Equipment	231,365.00	
146	Accum. Dep., Serv. & Shop Equip.		30,255.00
149	Trucks	62,850.00	
150	Accum. Depreciation, Trucks		3,950.00
153	Trailers	65,000.00	
154	Accum. Depreciation, Trailers		6,000.00
157	Office Equipment	12,010.00	
158	Accum. Deprec., Office Equip.		3,395.00
160	Leasehold	180,000.00	
165	Leasehold Improvements	400,000.00	
170	Patents	3,180.00	
175	Organization Costs	6,000.00	
201	Accounts Payable		198,215.30
203	Short-Term Notes Payable		270,000.00
204	Disc. on Short-Term Notes Pay.	3,025.00	
209	Salaries & Wages Payable		42,506.43
211	Sales Tax Payable		18,216.66
215	Unearned Moorage Fees		89,075.00
221	Employee's Federal Inc. Taxes Pay.		7,444.55
223	FICA Taxes Payable		8,275.58
225	State Unemployment Taxes Payable		555.22
227	Federal Unemployment Taxes Payable		185.07
235	Long-Term Lease Liability		6,000.00
236	Discount on Lease Financing	871.12	
241	Long-Term Notes Payable		105,000.00
242	Disc. on Long-Term Notes Pay.	8,125.00	
250	Bonds Payable		400,000.00
251	Discount on Bonds Payable	16,340.20	

Continued on next page

STUDENT DOCUMENTS FOR JUNE 23-30

Continued from previous page

	Accounts	Debit	Credit
301	Preferred Stock		100,000.00
303	Contrib. Cap. in Exc. of Par, Pref.		10,000.00
304	Contrib. Cap.--Retirement of Pref.		1,250.00
305	Common Stock		2,323,000.00
306	Common Stock Subscribed		100,000.00
308	Contrib. Cap. in Exc. of Par, Com.		117,515.00
315	Retained Earnings		110,024.86
320	Cash Dividends Declared	26,000.00	
325	Stock Dividends Declared	30,015.00	
330	Treasury Stock	27,050.00	
401	Houseboat Sales		1,253,777.78
407	Accessories & Parts Sales		41,310.00
408	Access. & Parts Sales Ret. & Allow.	370.00	
412	Service Fees Earned		58,869.56
420	Sales Commissions Earned		21,945.00
501	Purchases--Houseboats	1,456,000.00	
502	Purchases Discounts--Houseboats		21,890.00
503	Transportation-In--Houseboats	37,230.00	
505	Purchases--Accessories & Parts	21,967.29	
506	Purch. Ret. & Allow.--Acc. & Parts		1,225.00
507	Purch. Discounts--Access. & Parts		633.95
508	Transportation-In--Access. & Parts	320.00	
601	Office & Shop Salaries & Wages Exp.	106,188.77	
602	Executive & Salespersons Salaries	54,000.00	
604	Equipment Rental Expense	4,500.00	
607	Truck Operating Expense	3,103.80	
608	Advertising Expense	2,743.75	
609	Credit Card Expense	196.21	
610	Delivery Expense	96.17	
611	Tools Expense	197.08	
613	Deprec. Exp., Serv. & Shop Equip.	330.00	
615	Deprec. Expense, Trucks	750.00	
619	Deprec. Expense, Office Equipment	450.00	
621	Payroll Tax Expense	4,507.23	
625	Electric & Gas Expense	1,847.50	
626	Telephone Expense	1,403.70	
627	Bank Service Charges	61.00	
628	Cash Short and Over	8.00	
629	License Expense	1,407.50	
630	Professional Services Expense	1,440.00	
631	Janitorial Services Expense	966.50	
635	Miscellaneous Expense	91.62	

Continued on next page

STUDENT DOCUMENTS FOR JUNE 23-30

Continued from previous page

	Accounts	Debit	Credit
711	Interest Earned		7,751.37
713	Dividends Earned		6,432.00
715	Earnings on Investments		16,950.00
721	Gain on Sale of Assets		3,325.00
731	Gain on Short-Term Investments		10,957.00
741	Miscellaneous Revenue		76.00
811	Income Taxes Expense	31,500.00	
813	Interest Expense	17,427.46	
821	Loss on Sale/Disposal of Assets	250.00	
825	Loss on Retirement of Bonds	1,679.97	
831	Loss on Short-Term Investments	2,529.00	
835	Loss on Long-Term Investments	1,205.00	
Totals		$5,396,210.33	$5,396,210.33

STUDENT DOCUMENTS FOR JUNE 23-30

General Journal Entries

Date	Account	Ref	Debit	Credit
June 23	Service & Shop Supplies	131	146.88	
	Tools Expense	611	50.76	
	Accounts Payable	201		197.64
	Vendor: 25950			
	Invoice: Q3456			
June 24	Notes Receivable	109	15,000.00	
	Accounts Receivable	105		15,000.00
	Customer: 10200			
	Invoice: W2015			
June 24	Cash	101	102,366.18	
	Accounts Receivable	105		102,060.00
	Interest Earned	711		306.18
	Customer: 11405			
	Invoice: DISNT			
June 24	Truck Operating Expense	607	653.80	
	Cash	101		653.80
	Invoice: 55444			
	Check: 04024			
June 24	Cash	101	3,875.00	
	Sales Commissions Earned	420		3,875.00
	Invoice: CE602			
June 25	Common Stock Dividend Distrib.	307	23,000.00	
	Common Stock	305		23,000.00
	Invoice: STKDV			
June 26	Deprec. Exp., Serv. & Shop Equip.	613	30.00	
	Accum. Dep., Serv. & Shop Equip.	146		30.00
June 26	Service & Shop Equipment	145	39,520.00	
	Accum. Dep., Serv. & Shop Equip.	146	2,630.00	
	Service & Shop Equipment	145		4,950.00
	Cash	101		37,200.00
	Invoice: X3355			
	Check: 04025			

STUDENT DOCUMENTS FOR JUNE 23-30

General Journal Entries

Date	Account	Acct#	Debit	Credit
June 26	Electric & Gas Expense	625	535.50	
	Cash	101		535.50
	Invoice: 14388			
	Check: 04026			
June 26	Telephone Expense	626	499.70	
	Cash	101		499.70
	Invoice: 2555T			
	Check: 04028			
June 27	Accounts Payable	201	428,000.00	
	Cash	101		419,810.00
	Purchases Discounts--Houseboats	502		8,190.00
	Vendor: 22600			
	Invoice: K3556			
	Check: 04028			
June 28	Purchases--Houseboats	501	190,000.00	
	Cash	101		30,000.00
	Short-Term Notes Payable	203		160,000.00
	Invoice: 46005			
	Check: 04029			
June 28	Cash	101	106,975.00	
	Disc. on Short-Term Notes Pay.	204	3,025.00	
	Short-Term Notes Payable	203		110,000.00
	Invoice: NTPAY			
June 28	Accounts Payable	201	6,660.00	
	Cash	101		6,660.00
	Vendor: 21990			
	Invoice: F1466			
	Check: 04030			
June 29	Transportation-In--Houseboats	503	5,625.00	
	Cash	101		5,625.00
	Invoice: G4411			
	Check: 04031			
June 29	Cash Short and Over	628	1.00	
	Office Supplies	129	10.50	
	Miscellaneous Expense	635	17.50	
	Delivery Expense	610	16.50	
	Cash	101		45.50
	Invoice: PC601			
	Check: 04032			

STUDENT DOCUMENTS FOR JUNE 23-30

General Journal Entries

June 29	Cash	101	5,883.00	
	Notes Receivable	109		5,550.00
	Interest Earned	711		333.00
	Invoice: NTREC			
June 29	Cash	101	67.50	
	Interest Earned	711		67.50
	Invoice: BKINT			
June 30	Cash	101	6,000.00	
	Invest. in Baldwin Manufacturing	140		6,000.00
	Invoice: INVST			
June 30	Cash	101	1,698.00	
	Loss on Short-Term Investments	831	2,394.00	
	Short-Term Investments	103		4,092.00
	Invoice: INVST			
June 30	Long-Term Notes Payable	241	10,000.00	
	Interest Expense	813	2,362.50	
	Cash	101		12,362.50
	Invoice: NTPAY			
	Check: 04033			
June 30	Office & Shop Salaries & Wages Exp.	601	36,088.77	
	Executive & Salespersons Salaries	602	18,000.00	
	Employee's Federal Inc. Taxes Pay.	221		7,444.55
	FICA Taxes Payable	223		4,137.79
	Salaries & Wages Payable	209		42,506.43
	Invoice: PAYRL			
June 30	Payroll Tax Expense	621	4,507.23	
	FICA Taxes Payable	223		4,137.79
	State Unemployment Taxes Payable	225		277.08
	Federal Unemployment Taxes Payable	227		92.36
	Invoice: EMPTX			

STUDENT DOCUMENTS FOR JUNE 23-30

General Journal Entries

Date	Account	Acct#	Debit	Credit
June 30	Long-Term Lease Liability	235	500.00	
	Cash	101		500.00
	Invoice: LEASE			
	Check: 04034			
June 30	Interest Expense	813	137.29	
	Discount on Lease Financing	236		137.29
June 30	Preferred Stock	301	100,000.00	
	Contrib. Cap. in Exc. of Par, Pref.	303	10,000.00	
	Cash	101		108,750.00
	Contrib. Cap.--Retirement of Pref.	304		1,250.00
	Invoice: RSTOK			
	Check: 04035			
June 30	Cash	101	6,350.00	
	Unearned Moorage Fees	215		6,350.00
	Invoice: MF062			
June 30	Purchases--Houseboats	501	180,000.00	
	Accounts Payable	201		180,000.00
	Vendor: 27125			
	Invoice: L5311			
June 30	Accounts Payable	201	1,125.00	
	Purch. Ret. & Allow.--Acc. & Parts	506		1,125.00
	Vendor: 28400			
	Invoice: T3555			
	Debit Memo: DM002			

STUDENT DOCUMENTS

FOR THE

END OF THE SECOND QUARTER

JUNE 30, 1993

The student is required to print all of the documents shown in this section except the General Journal.

STUDENT DOCUMENTS
FOR THE END OF THE SECOND QUARTER, JUNE 30, 1997

```
                    Wild Goose Marina, Incorporated
                         Adjusted Trial Balance
                              June 30, 1997
```

	Accounts	Debit	Credit
101	Cash	$ 174,707.65	
102	Petty Cash	100.00	
103	Short-Term Investments	119,999.50	
105	Accounts Receivable	79,969.76	
106	Allowance for Doubtful Accounts		$ 2,475.00
109	Notes Receivable	221,500.00	
113	Interest Receivable	2,780.76	
116	Subscriptions Rec., Common Stock	92,400.00	
117	Merch. Inventory--Houseboats	785,330.00	
119	Merch. Inventory--Access.& Parts	34,200.00	
123	Prepaid Insurance	14,775.00	
124	Prepaid Rent	12,000.00	
127	Prepaid Advertising	235.00	
129	Office Supplies	549.50	
131	Service & Shop Supplies	1,441.13	
140	Invest. in Baldwin Manufacturing	218,509.70	
141	Long-Term Investments	1,255,955.50	
145	Service & Shop Equipment	231,365.00	
146	Accum. Dep., Serv. & Shop Equip.		35,705.00
149	Trucks	62,850.00	
150	Accum. Depreciation, Trucks		5,652.00
153	Trailers	65,000.00	
154	Accum. Depreciation, Trailers		7,500.00
157	Office Equipment	12,010.00	
158	Accum. Deprec., Office Equip.		4,240.00
160	Leasehold	174,375.00	
165	Leasehold Improvements	389,843.75	
170	Patents	2,981.25	
175	Organization Costs	5,625.00	
201	Accounts Payable		198,215.30
202	Interest Payable		1,273.34
203	Short-Term Notes Payable		270,000.00
204	Disc. on Short-Term Notes Pay.	2,957.78	
209	Salaries & Wages Payable		42,506.43
211	Sales Tax Payable		18,216.66
212	Estimated Property Taxes Payable		630.00
213	Income Taxes Payable		956.00
215	Unearned Moorage Fees		38,825.00
221	Employee's Federal Inc. Taxes Pay.		7,444.55
223	FICA Taxes Payable		8,275.58
225	State Unemployment Taxes Payable		555.22
227	Federal Unemployment Taxes Payable		185.07
235	Long-Term Lease Liability		6,000.00
236	Discount on Lease Financing	871.12	
241	Long-Term Notes Payable		105,000.00
242	Disc. on Long-Term Notes Pay.	7,967.50	
250	Bonds Payable		400,000.00
251	Discount on Bonds Payable	16,228.00	

Continued on next page

STUDENT DOCUMENTS
FOR THE END OF THE SECOND QUARTER, JUNE 30, 1997

Continued from previous page

	Accounts	Debit	Credit
301	Preferred Stock		100,000.00
303	Contrib. Cap. in Exc. of Par, Pref.		10,000.00
304	Contrib. Cap.--Retirement of Pref.		1,250.00
305	Common Stock		2,323,000.00
306	Common Stock Subscribed		100,000.00
308	Contrib. Cap. in Exc. of Par, Com.		117,515.00
315	Retained Earnings		110,024.86
320	Cash Dividends Declared	26,000.00	
325	Stock Dividends Declared	30,015.00	
330	Treasury Stock	27,050.00	
401	Houseboat Sales		1,253,777.78
407	Accessories & Parts Sales		41,310.00
408	Access. & Parts Sales Ret. & Allow.	370.00	
412	Service Fees Earned		58,869.56
415	Moorage Fees Earned		50,250.00
420	Sales Commissions Earned		21,945.00
501	Purchases--Houseboats	1,456,000.00	
502	Purchases Discounts--Houseboats		21,890.00
503	Transportation-In--Houseboats	37,230.00	
505	Purchases--Accessories & Parts	21,967.29	
506	Purch. Ret. & Allow.--Acc. & Parts		1,225.00
507	Purch. Discounts--Access. & Parts		633.95
508	Transportation-In--Access. & Parts	320.00	
601	Office & Shop Salaries & Wages Exp.	106,188.77	
602	Executive & Salespersons Salaries	54,000.00	
603	Rent Expense	27,781.25	
604	Equipment Rental Expense	4,500.00	
605	Office Supplies Expense	1,082.97	
606	Service & Shop Supplies Expense	1,413.75	
607	Truck Operating Expense	3,103.80	
608	Advertising Expense	2,508.75	
609	Credit Card Expense	196.21	
610	Delivery Expense	96.17	
611	Tools Expense	197.08	
613	Deprec. Exp., Serv. & Shop Equip.	5,780.00	
615	Deprec. Expense, Trucks	2,452.00	
617	Deprec. Expense, Trailers	1,500.00	
619	Deprec. Expense, Office Equipment	1,295.00	
621	Payroll Tax Expense	4,507.23	
622	Insurance Expense	6,875.00	
623	Bad Debt Expense	2,271.00	
624	Property Tax Expense	630.00	
625	Electric & Gas Expense	1,847.50	
626	Telephone Expense	1,403.70	
627	Bank Service Charges	61.00	
628	Cash Short and Over	8.00	
629	License Expense	1,407.50	
630	Professional Services Expense	1,440.00	
631	Janitorial Services Expense	966.50	
632	Amortization Expense--Patents	198.75	
633	Amortiz. Expense--Organiz. Costs	375.00	
635	Miscellaneous Expense	91.62	

Continued on next page

STUDENT DOCUMENTS
FOR THE END OF THE SECOND QUARTER, JUNE 30, 1997

Continued from previous page

	Accounts	Debit	Credit
711	Interest Earned		10,532.13
713	Dividends Earned		6,432.00
715	Earnings on Investments		16,950.00
721	Gain on Sale of Assets		3,325.00
731	Gain on Short-Term Investments		10,957.00
741	Miscellaneous Revenue		76.00
811	Income Taxes Expense	32,456.00	
813	Interest Expense	19,037.72	
821	Loss on Sale/Disposal of Assets	250.00	
825	Loss on Retirement of Bonds	1,679.97	
831	Loss on Short-Term Investments	2,529.00	
835	Loss on Long-Term Investments	1,205.00	
901	Income Summary		463,198.00
Totals		$5,876,816.43	$5,876,816.43

STUDENT DOCUMENTS
FOR THE END OF THE SECOND QUARTER, JUNE 30, 1997

```
            Wild Goose Marina, Incorporated
         Series Two Bonds Discount Amortization Schedule
           Par Value: $400,000   Term: 5 years
                   Interest Paid Quarterly
             Bond Interest: 7%   Market Rate: 8%
```

Time Periods	Interest Paid	Interest Recognized	Amortization of Discount	Unamortized Discount	Carrying Amount of Bond
1	$7,000.00	$7,673.20	$673.20	$15,667.00	$384,333.00
2	7,000.00	7,686.66	686.66	14,980.34	385,019.66
3	7,000.00	7,700.39	700.39	14,279.95	385,720.05
4	7,000.00	7,714.40	714.40	13,565.55	386,434.45

STUDENT DOCUMENTS
FOR THE END OF THE SECOND QUARTER, JUNE 30, 1997

General Journal Entries

June 30	Office Supplies Expense	605	1,082.97	
	Office Supplies	129		1,082.97
	Adjusting Entry			
June 30	Service & Shop Supplies Expense	606	1,413.75	
	Service & Shop Supplies	131		1,413.75
	Adjusting Entry			
June 30	Insurance Expense	622	6,875.00	
	Prepaid Insurance	123		6,875.00
	Adjusting Entry			
June 30	Prepaid Advertising	127	235.00	
	Advertising Expense	608		235.00
	Adjusting Entry			
June 30	Property Tax Expense	624	630.00	
	Estimated Property Taxes Payable	212		630.00
	Adjusting Entry			
June 30	Deprec. Exp., Serv. & Shop Equip.	613	5,450.00	
	Accum. Dep., Serv. & Shop Equip.	146		5,450.00
	Adjusting Entry			
June 30	Deprec. Expense, Trucks	615	1,702.00	
	Accum. Depreciation, Trucks	150		1,702.00
	Adjusting Entry			
June 30	Deprec. Expense, Trailers	617	1,500.00	
	Accum. Depreciation, Trailers	154		1,500.00
	Adjusting Entry			
June 30	Deprec. Expense, Office Equipment	619	845.00	
	Accum. Deprec., Office Equip.	158		845.00
	Adjusting Entry			
June 30	Interest Receivable	113	2,780.76	
	Interest Earned	711		2,780.76
	Adjusting Entry			

STUDENT DOCUMENTS
FOR THE END OF THE SECOND QUARTER, JUNE 30, 1997

General Journal Entries

Date	Account	No.	Debit	Credit
June 30	Unearned Moorage Fees	215	50,250.00	
	Moorage Fees Earned	415		50,250.00
	Adjusting Entry			
June 30	Income Taxes Expense	811	956.00	
	Income Taxes Payable	213		956.00
	Adjusting Entry			
June 30	Rent Expense	603	5,625.00	
	Leasehold	160		5,625.00
	Adjusting Entry			
June 30	Rent Expense	603	10,156.25	
	Leasehold Improvements	165		10,156.25
	Adjusting Entry			
June 30	Bad Debt Expense	623	2,271.00	
	Allowance for Doubtful Accounts	106		2,271.00
	Adjusting Entry			
June 30	Rent Expense	603	12,000.00	
	Prepaid Rent	124		12,000.00
	Adjusting Entry			
June 30	Amortization Expense--Patents	632	198.75	
	Patents	170		198.75
	Adjusting Entry			
June 30	Amortiz. Expense--Organiz. Costs	633	375.00	
	Organization Costs	175		375.00
	Adjusting Entry			
June 30	Interest Expense	813	106.67	
	Interest Payable	202		106.67
	Adjusting Entry			
June 30	Interest Expense	813	67.22	
	Disc. on Short-Term Notes Pay.	204		67.22
	Adjusting Entry			

STUDENT DOCUMENTS
FOR THE END OF THE SECOND QUARTER, JUNE 30, 1997

General Journal Entries

Date	Account	No.	Debit	Credit
June 30	Interest Expense	813	157.50	
	Disc. on Long-Term Notes Pay.	242		157.50
	Adjusting Entry			
June 30	Interest Expense	813	1,278.87	
	Interest Payable	202		1,166.67
	Discount on Bonds Payable	251		112.20
	Adjusting Entry			
June 30	Income Summary	901	356,332.00	
	Merch. Inventory--Houseboats	117		315,200.00
	Merch. Inventory--Access.& Parts	119		41,132.00
	Adjusting Entry			
June 30	Merch. Inventory--Houseboats	117	785,330.00	
	Merch. Inventory--Access.& Parts	119	34,200.00	
	Income Summary	901		819,530.00
	Adjusting Entry			

STUDENT DOCUMENTS
FOR THE END OF THE SECOND QUARTER, JUNE 30, 1997

Wild Goose Marina, Incorporated
Income Statement
For the Quarter Ended June 30, 1997

Revenues:		
Houseboat sales	$ 1,253,777.78	
Cost of goods sold--houseboats	1,001,210.00	
Gross margin--houseboat sales		$ 252,567.78
Assec. & parts sales (net)	$ 40,940.00	
Cost of goods sold--accessories & parts	27,360.34	
Gross margin--accessories & parts sales		13,579.66
Service fees earned	$ 58,869.56	
Moorage fees earned	50,250.00	
Sales commissions earned	21,945.00	
Total fees and commissions earned		131,064.56
Total gross margin from operations		$ 397,212.00
Operating Expenses:		
Office & shop salaries & wages exp.	$ 106,188.77	
Executive & salespersons salaries	54,000.00	
Rent expense	27,781.25	
Equipment rental expense	4,500.00	
Office supplies expense	1,082.97	
Service & shop supplies expense	1,413.75	
Truck operating expense	3,103.80	
Advertising expense	2,508.75	
Credit card expense	196.21	
Delivery expense	96.17	
Tools expense	197.08	
Deprec. exp., serv. & shop equip.	5,780.00	
Deprec. expense, trucks	2,452.00	
Deprec. expense, trailers	1,500.00	
Deprec. expense, office equipment	1,295.00	
Payroll tax expense	4,507.23	
Insurance expense	6,875.00	
Bad debt expense	2,271.00	
Property tax expense	630.00	
Electric & gas expense	1,847.50	
Telephone expense	1,403.70	
Bank service charges	61.00	
Cash short and over	8.00	
License expense	1,407.50	
Professional services expense	1,440.00	
Janitorial services expense	966.50	
Amortization expense--patents	198.75	
Amortiz. expense--organiz. costs	375.00	
Miscellaneous expense	91.62	
Total operating expenses		234,178.55
Income from operations		$ 163,033.45

Income Statement continued on next page...

STUDENT DOCUMENTS
FOR THE END OF THE SECOND QUARTER, JUNE 30, 1997

Income Statement continued...

```
Other revenues and expenses:
  Other revenues:
    Interest earned                  $  10,532.13
    Dividends earned                     6,432.00
    Earnings on investments             16,950.00
    Gain on sale of assets               3,325.00
    Gain on short-term investments      10,957.00
    Miscellaneous revenue                   76.00   $  48,272.13
                                     ----------

  Other expenses:
    Income taxes expense             $  32,456.00
    Interest expense                    19,037.72
    Loss on sale/disposal of assets        250.00
    Loss on retirement of bonds          1,679.97
    Loss on short-term investments       2,529.00
    Loss on long-term investments        1,205.00      57,157.69
                                     ----------   ------------

      Net other expenses                                            8,885.56
                                                                ----------
Net income                                                       $ 154,147.89
                                                                ==========
```

```
                    Wild Goose Marina, Incorporated
                       Retained Earnings Statement
                     For the Quarter Ended June 30, 1997

Retained earnings, March 31, 1997                              $ 110,724.86

    Add:   Net income                      $ 154,147.89

    Less:  Cash dividends declared            26,000.00
           Stock dividends declared           30,015.00
           Other deductions                      700.00
                                          ----------
    Net increase in retained earnings                              97,432.89
                                                                ----------
Retained earnings, June 30, 1997                               $ 208,157.75
                                                                ==========
```

STUDENT DOCUMENTS
FOR THE END OF THE SECOND QUARTER, JUNE 30, 1997

```
                   Wild Goose Marina, Incorporated
                            Balance Sheet
                            June 30, 1997

                               ASSETS

Current assets:
  Cash                                                  $   174,707.65
  Petty cash                                                    100.00
  Short-term investments                                    119,999.50
  Accounts receivable                    $  79,969.76
  Allowance for doubtful accounts            2,475.00
                                         ----------
  Net accounts receivable                                    77,494.76
  Notes receivable                                          221,500.00
  Interest receivable                                         2,780.76
  Subscriptions rec., common stock                           92,400.00
  Merch. inventory--houseboats                              785,330.00
  Merch. inventory--access.& parts                           34,200.00
  Prepaid insurance                                          14,775.00
  Prepaid rent                                               12,000.00
  Prepaid advertising                                           235.00
  Office supplies                                               549.50
  Service & shop supplies                                     1,441.13
                                                         ----------
Total current assets                                                     $ 1,537,513.30

Investments:
  Invest. in baldwin manufacturing                       $  218,509.70
  Long-term investments                                   1,255,955.50
  Bond sinking fund                                               0.00
                                                         ----------
Total Investments                                                          1,474,465.20

Plant and equipment:
  Service & shop equipment               $ 231,365.00
  Accum. dep., serv. & shop equip.          35,705.00
                                         ----------
    Book Value                                          $   195,660.00
  Trucks                                 $  62,850.00
  Accum. depreciation, trucks                5,652.00
                                         ----------
    Book Value                                          $    57,198.00
  Trailers                               $  65,000.00
  Accum. depreciation, trailers              7,500.00
                                         ----------
    Book Value                                          $    57,500.00
  Office equipment                       $  12,010.00
  Accum. deprec., office equip.              4,240.00
                                         ----------
    Book Value                                          $     7,770.00
                                                         ----------
Total plant and equipment                                                    318,128.00
```

STUDENT DOCUMENTS
FOR THE END OF THE SECOND QUARTER, JUNE 30, 1997

Balance Sheet continued

Intangible assets:			
Leasehold		$ 174,375.00	
Leasehold improvements		389,843.75	
Patents		2,981.25	
Organization costs		5,625.00	
Total intangible assets			572,825.00
Total assets			$ 3,902,931.50

LIABILITIES

Current liabilities:			
Accounts payable		$ 198,215.30	
Interest payable		1,273.34	
Short-term notes payable	$ 270,000.00		
Disc. on short-term notes pay.	2,957.78	267,042.22	
Current portion of long-term notes		40,000.00	
Legal fees payable		0.00	
Preferred cash dividends payable		0.00	
Common cash dividends payable		0.00	
Salaries & wages payable		42,506.43	
Sales tax payable		18,216.66	
Estimated property taxes payable		630.00	
Income taxes payable		956.00	
Unearned moorage fees		38,825.00	
Employee's federal inc. taxes pay.		7,444.55	
Fica taxes payable		8,275.58	
State unemployment taxes payable		555.22	
Federal unemployment taxes payable		185.07	
Total current liabilities			$ 584,125.37
Long-term liabilities:			
Long-term lease liability	$ 6,000.00		
Discount on lease financing	871.12		
Carrying value of long-term lease		$ 5,128.88	
Long-term notes payable	$ 65,000.00		
Disc. on long-term notes pay.	7,967.50		
Carrying value of long-term notes		57,032.50	
Bonds payable	$ 400,000.00		
Discount on bonds payable	16,228.00		
Carrying value of bonds		383,772.00	
Total Long-term liabilities			485,933.38
Total liabilities			$ 1,070,058.75

STUDENT DOCUMENTS
FOR THE END OF THE SECOND QUARTER, JUNE 30, 1997

Balance Sheet continued

STOCKHOLDERS' EQUITY

Preferred stock	$ 100,000.00	
Contrib. cap. in exc. of par, pref.	10,000.00	
Contrib. cap.--retirement of pref.	1,250.00	
Total contributed capital, preferred stock	$ 111,250.00	
Common stock	$ 2,323,000.00	
Common stock subscribed	100,000.00	
Contrib. cap. in exc. of par, com.	117,515.00	
Total contributed capital, common stock	$ 2,540,515.00	
Contrib. cap.--treas. stock trans.	$ 0.00	
Total contributed capital		$ 2,651,765.00
Retained earnings		208,157.75
Total		$ 2,859,922.75
Less Treasury stock		27,050.00
Total stockholders' equity		$ 2,832,872.75
Total liabilities and stockholders' equity		$ 3,902,931.50

STUDENT DOCUMENTS
FOR THE END OF THE SECOND QUARTER, JUNE 30, 1997

```
                  Wild Goose Marina, Incorporated
                  Schedule of Accounts Receivable
                            June 30, 1997
```

Customer Number	Customer Name	Account Balance
10200	Adams Farms Incorporated	$ 0.00
10550	Bettencourt, Inc.	58,346.76
10820	R. J. Corsetti	1,988.00
11050	J. P. Elam	0.00
11185	Joan Kuhlman	0.00
11260	Kingston & Sons, Inc.	6,210.00
11350	Dale Novice	0.00
11405	Randy Robberts	0.00
11470	Roseburg & Associates	13,425.00
11520	Taylor Company	0.00
11695	Tisedaile Const. Co.	0.00
11920	Zakk, Incorporated	0.00
Totals		$ 79,969.76

STUDENT DOCUMENTS
FOR THE END OF THE SECOND QUARTER, JUNE 30, 1997

Accounts Receivable Subsidiary Ledger

Page 1

Adams Farms Incorporated
3354 East Avenue
Placerville, CA   No. 10200

  Date   Description   Debit   Credit   Balance

  May 25   W2015   15,000.00   15,000.00
  June 23   W2015   15,000.00   0.00

Bettencourt, Inc.
8000 Baywood Street
Sacramento, CA   No. 10550

  Date   Description   Debit   Credit   Balance

  May 28   W2024   57,000.00   57,000.00
  June 4   W2032   1,346.76   58,346.76

R. J. Corsetti
6677 Hill Road
Auburn, CA   No. 10820

  Date   Description   Debit   Credit   Balance

  May 17   W1995   2,150.00   2,150.00
  June 14   CM201   W1995   162.00   1,988.00

J. P. Elam
6525 Carolinda Dr.
Forest Hill, CA   No. 11050

  Date   Description   Debit   Credit   Balance

  Jan. 1   W1760   432.00   432.00
  Apr. 20   W1760   WROFF   432.00   0.00
  June 9   RECOV   432.00   432.00
  June 9   RECOV   432.00   0.00
  June 14   BADCK   4,016.00   4,016.00
  June 18   W2035   4,016.00   0.00

Continued next page...

STUDENT DOCUMENTS
FOR THE END OF THE SECOND QUARTER, JUNE 30, 1997

Accounts Receivable Subsidiary Ledger   Page 2

Joan Kuhlman
4588 Gold Run Road
Malibu, CA   No. 11185

Date	Description	Debit	Credit	Balance
June 1	Beginning Balance			0.00

Kingston & Sons, Inc.
456 Snowcrest Court
Fair Oaks, CA   No. 11260

Date	Description	Debit	Credit	Balance
June 1	Beginning Balance			0.00
June 9	W2033	6,210.00		6,210.00

Dale Novice
5550 Rock Road
Oakland, CA   No. 11350

Date	Description	Debit	Credit	Balance
Feb. 1	W1805	550.00		550.00
June 7	WROFF		550.00	0.00

Randy Robberts
456 GEO Drive
Grass Valley, CA   No. 11405

Date	Description	Debit	Credit	Balance
June 1	Beginning Balance			0.00
June 16	DISHO	102,060.00		102,060.00
June 24	DISNT		102,060.00	0.00

Continued next page...

STUDENT DOCUMENTS
FOR THE END OF THE SECOND QUARTER, JUNE 30, 1997

Accounts Receivable Subsidiary Ledger   Page 3

Roseburg & Associates
444 3rd Ave. Suite B
Yuba City, CA   No. 11470

Date	Description	Debit	Credit	Balance
June 1	Beginning Balance			0.00
June 22	W2037	13,425.00		13,425.00

Taylor Company
5162 Brook Court
Clayton, CA   No. 11520

Date	Description	Debit	Credit	Balance
Jan. 1	W1761	2,670.00		2,670.00
June 19	WROFF		2,670.00	0.00

Tisedaile Const. Co.
123 Ball Court
Hoop, OR   No. 11695

Date	Description	Debit	Credit	Balance
May 4	W1955	42,251.75		42,251.75
June 4	W1995		42,251.75	0.00

Zakk, Incorporated
1313 Pine Drive
Granite Bay, CA   No. 11920

Date	Description	Debit	Credit	Balance
May 1	W1950	6,500.00		6,500.00
June 4	NTREC		6,500.00	0.00

STUDENT DOCUMENTS
FOR THE END OF THE SECOND QUARTER, JUNE 30, 1997

```
              Wild Goose Marina, Incorporated
               Schedule of Accounts Payable
                      June 30, 1997
```

Vendor Number	Vendor Name	Account Balance
20500	Corr Marine Supply	$ 0.00
21990	Foster Business Supply	0.00
22600	Kruzer Houseboats	0.00
24800	Luzzi, Incorporated	0.00
25950	Quinlivin, Incorporated	197.64
26675	Reading Real Estate	0.00
27005	Rockwood Business Supply	537.97
27125	Snow Goose Houseboats	190,500.00
28400	Yee & Associates, Inc.	6,979.69
Totals		$ 198,215.30

STUDENT DOCUMENTS
FOR THE END OF THE SECOND QUARTER, JUNE 30, 1997

Accounts Payable Subsidiary Ledger

Page 1

Corr Marine Supply
4455 Stone Court
    Loomis, CA   1/15, n/30   No. 20500

Date	Description	Debit	Credit	Balance
May 26	C6211		13,650.00	13,650.00
June 11	C6211 04008	13,650.00		0.00

Foster Business Supply
5114 Santa Clara
    Anderson, CA   2/10, n/30   No. 21990

Date	Description	Debit	Credit	Balance
May 29	F1466		6,660.00	6,660.00
June 28	F1466 04030	6,660.00		0.00

Kruzer Houseboats
6666 Pontoon Way
    Redding, CA   2/10, n/30   No. 22600

Date	Description	Debit	Credit	Balance
May 28	K2244		260,000.00	260,000.00
June 7	K2244 04005	260,000.00		0.00
June 17	K3556		428,000.00	428,000.00
June 27	K3556 04028	428,000.00		0.00

Luzzi, Incorporated
690 Fairhaven Court
    Rio Linda, CA   Net 10   No. 24800

Date	Description	Debit	Credit	Balance
Beginning Balance				0.00
June 1	L2556		864.00	864.00
June 12	L2256 04009	864.00		0.00

Continued next page...

STUDENT DOCUMENTS
FOR THE END OF THE SECOND QUARTER, JUNE 30, 1997

```
Accounts Payable Subsidiary Ledger                         Page   2

Quinlivin, Incorporated
5555 Firecrst Road
  Colfax, Ca      Net 30                                   No. 25950
-------------------------------------------------------------------
   Date         Description        Debit       Credit      Balance
-------------------------------------------------------------------
Beginning Balance                                              0.00
  June 23    Q3456                              197.64       197.64
-------------------------------------------------------------------


Reading Real Estate
4005 Magnolia Ave.
  Sacramento, CA  2/10, n/30                               No. 26675
-------------------------------------------------------------------
   Date         Description        Debit       Credit      Balance
-------------------------------------------------------------------
Beginning Balance                                              0.00
-------------------------------------------------------------------


Rockwood Business Supply
2105 Baylor Road
  Auburn, CA     Net 30                                    No. 27005
-------------------------------------------------------------------
   Date         Description        Debit       Credit      Balance
-------------------------------------------------------------------
Beginning Balance                                              0.00
  June 13    55663                              566.22       566.22
  June 14    55663                 28.25                     537.97
-------------------------------------------------------------------


Snow Goose Houseboats
111 Cackler Circle
  Honker Bay, WA Net 30                                    No. 27125
-------------------------------------------------------------------
   Date         Description        Debit       Credit      Balance
-------------------------------------------------------------------
Beginning Balance                                              0.00
  June  2    S3344                           10,500.00    10,500.00
  June 30    L5311                          180,000.00   190,500.00
-------------------------------------------------------------------
```

Continued next page...

STUDENT DOCUMENTS
FOR THE END OF THE SECOND QUARTER, JUNE 30, 1997

Accounts Payable Subsidiary Ledger   Page 3

Yee & Associates, Inc.
4436 Bayye Street
  Rocklin, CA   Net 30   No. 28400

     Date   Description   Debit   Credit   Balance

Beginning Balance   0.00
  June 20   T3555   8,104.69   8,104.69
  June 30   T3555   DM002   1,125.00   6,979.69

STUDENT DOCUMENTS
FOR THE END OF THE SECOND QUARTER, JUNE 30, 1997

General Ledger Account

CASH   Acct. No. 101

Date	Description			Debit	Credit	Balance
June 1	Beginning Balance					226,015.23
June 1	W2030			106.92		226,122.15
June 1	22334		03999		19.75	226,102.40
June 2				19.75		226,122.15
June 2	22334		ERROR		19.75	226,102.40
June 2	INTPA		04000		6,000.00	220,102.40
June 2	BONDR		04001		206,000.00	14,102.40
June 3	W2031			148,500.00		162,602.40
June 3	PAYRL		04002		39,355.23	123,247.17
June 4	LRENT		04003		1,500.00	121,747.17
June 4	W1995	11695		42,251.75		163,998.92
June 5	W1901			10,600.00		174,598.92
June 5	DIVPA		04004		25,600.00	148,998.92
June 6	DISNT			142,243.50		291,242.42
June 7	K2244	22600	04005		254,800.00	36,442.42
June 8	SUBRE			122,250.00		158,692.42
June 8	FEDTX		04006		15,362.50	143,329.92
June 8	CSTOK			128,500.00		271,829.92
June 8	CASHD			3,800.00		275,629.92
June 9	RECOV	11050		432.00		276,061.92
June 9	CE601			2,970.00		279,031.92
June 9	STOKS			28,682.50		307,714.42
June 10	ASALE			350.00		308,064.42
June 10	HF244		04007		624.00	307,440.42
June 11	C6211	20500	04008		13,513.50	293,926.92
June 11	L2256	24800	04009		864.00	293,062.92
June 12	TSTOK		04010		40,575.00	252,487.92
June 13	W2034			2,268.00		254,755.92
June 13	W2035			3,996.00		258,751.92
June 13	CASHD			520.00		259,271.92
June 14	W2030	11050	BADCK		3,996.00	255,275.92
June 15	Q1521		04011		17.55	255,258.37
June 15	EXTRA		04012		9,550.00	245,708.37
June 15	BONDS			383,659.80		629,368.17
June 15	MF061			10,175.00		639,543.17
June 15	INCTX		04013		31,500.00	608,043.17
June 16	INVST		04014		5,955.50	602,087.67
June 16	W1855	11405	DISHO		102,060.00	500,027.67
June 17	TSTOK			12,825.00		512,852.67
June 17	SALTX		04015		29,862.38	482,990.29
June 17	ASALE			2,600.00		485,590.29
June 18	W2035	11050		4,016.00		489,606.29
June 18	12655		04016		354.50	489,251.79
June 18	SS301		04017		825.00	488,426.79
June 19	WROFF	11520		575.00		489,001.79
June 19	SUBRE			39,600.00		528,601.79

Continued on next page...

STUDENT DOCUMENTS
FOR THE END OF THE SECOND QUARTER, JUNE 30, 1997

```
                        General Ledger Account
       CASH                                              Acct. No. 101
```

Date	Description			Debit	Credit	Balance
June 19	DP651		04018		1,200.00	527,401.79
June 19	DISNT		04019		90,000.00	437,401.79
June 20	11334		04020		71.32	437,330.47
June 21	W2036			232,500.00		669,830.47
June 22	N1566		04021		30,000.00	639,830.47
June 22	DMV06		04022		695.50	639,134.97
June 22	G7777		04023		75,000.00	564,134.97
June 24	DISNT	11405		102,366.18		666,501.15
June 24	55444		04024		653.80	665,847.35
June 24	CE602			3,875.00		669,722.35
June 26	X3355		04025		37,200.00	632,522.35
June 26	14388		04026		535.50	631,986.85
June 26	2555T		04027		499.70	631,487.15
June 27	K3556	22600	04028		419,810.00	211,677.15
June 28	46005		04029		30,000.00	181,677.15
June 28	NTPAY			106,975.00		288,652.15
June 28	F1466	21990	04030		6,660.00	281,992.15
June 29	G4411		04031		5,625.00	276,367.15
June 29	PC601		04032		45.50	276,321.65
June 29	NTREC			5,883.00		282,204.65
June 29	BKINT			67.50		282,272.15
June 30	INVST			6,000.00		288,272.15
June 30	INVST			1,698.00		289,970.15
June 30	INSNT		04033		12,362.50	277,607.65
June 30	LEASE		04034		500.00	277,107.65
June 30	RSTOK		04035		108,750.00	168,357.65
June 30	MF062			6,350.00		174,707.65

STUDENT DOCUMENTS
FOR THE END OF THE SECOND QUARTER, JUNE 30, 1997

General Ledger Account
ACCOUNTS RECEIVABLE — Acct. No. 105

Date	Description			Debit	Credit	Balance
June 1	Beginning Balance					126,121.75
June 4	W2032	10550		1,346.76		127,468.51
June 4	W1995	11695			42,251.75	85,216.76
June 4	NTREC	11920			6,500.00	78,716.76
June 7	WROFF	11350			550.00	78,166.76
June 9	RECOV	11050		432.00		78,598.76
June 9	RECOV	11050			432.00	78,166.76
June 9	W2033	11260		6,210.00		84,376.76
June 14	W1995	10820	CM201		162.00	84,214.76
June 14	W2030	11050	BADCK	4,016.00		88,230.76
June 16	W1855	11405	DISHO	102,060.00		190,290.76
June 18	W2035	11050			4,016.00	186,274.76
June 19	WROFF	11520			2,670.00	183,604.76
June 22	W2037	11470		13,425.00		197,029.76
June 24	W2015	10200			15,000.00	182,029.76
June 24	DISNT	11405			102,060.00	79,969.76

General Ledger Account
MERCH. INVENTORY--HOUSEBOATS — Acct. No. 117

Date	Description	Debit	Credit	Balance
June 1	Beginning Balance			315,200.00
June 30	Adjusting		315,200.00	0.00
June 30	Adjusting	785,330.00		785,330.00

General Ledger Account
INVEST. IN BALDWIN MANUFACTURING — Acct. No. 140

Date	Description	Debit	Credit	Balance
June 1	Beginning Balance			207,559.70
June 21	EARNS	16,950.00		224,509.70
June 30	INVST		6,000.00	218,509.70

STUDENT DOCUMENTS
FOR THE END OF THE SECOND QUARTER, JUNE 30, 1997

General Ledger Account

ACCOUNTS PAYABLE   Acct. No. 201

Date	Description			Debit	Credit	Balance
June 1	Beginning Balance					280,310.00
June 2	L2556	24800			864.00	281,174.00
June 2	S3344	27125			10,500.00	291,674.00
June 7	K2244	22600	04005	260,000.00		31,674.00
June 11	C6211	20500	04008	13,650.00		18,024.00
June 12	L2256	24800	04009	864.00		17,160.00
June 13	55663	27005			566.22	17,726.22
June 14	55663	27005		28.25		17,697.97
June 17	K3556	22600			428,000.00	445,697.97
June 20	T3555	28400			8,104.69	453,802.66
June 24	Q3456	25950			197.64	454,000.30
June 27	K3556	22600	04028	428,000.00		26,000.30
June 28	F1466	21990	04030	6,660.00		19,340.30
June 30	L5311	27125			180,000.00	199,340.30
June 30	T3555	28400	DM002	1,125.00		198,215.30

General Ledger Account

RETAINED EARNINGS   Acct. No. 315

Date	Description	Debit	Credit	Balance
June 1	Beginning Balance			110,724.86
June 17	TSTOK	700.00		110,024.86
June 30	Closing		154,147.89	264,172.75
June 30	Closing	26,000.00		238,172.75
June 30	Closing	30,015.00		208,157.75

General Ledger Account

TREASURY STOCK   Acct. No. 330

Date	Description		Debit	Credit	Balance
June 1	Beginning Balance				0.00
June 12	TSTOK	04010	40,575.00		40,575.00
June 17	TSTOK			13,525.00	27,050.00

STUDENT DOCUMENTS
FOR THE END OF THE SECOND QUARTER, JUNE 30, 1997

```
                         General Ledger Account
     HOUSEBOAT SALES                                      Acct. No. 401
    -----------------------------------------------------------------------
     Date         Description          Debit          Credit       Balance
    -----------------------------------------------------------------------
     June  1    Beginning Balance                                 901,000.00
     June  3    W2031                              137,500.00   1,038,500.00
     June 21    W2036                              215,277.78   1,253,777.78
     June 30    Closing              1,253,777.78                       0.00

    =======================================================================


                         General Ledger Account
     INCOME SUMMARY                                       Acct. No. 901
    -----------------------------------------------------------------------
     Date         Description          Debit          Credit       Balance
    -----------------------------------------------------------------------
     June  1    Beginning Balance                                       0.00
     June 30    Adjusting              356,332.00               356,332.00
     June 30    Adjusting                             819,530.00 463,198.00
     June 30    Closing                463,198.00                     0.00
     June 30    Closing                            1,961,371.42 1,961,371.42
     June 30    Closing              1,807,223.53               154,147.89
     June 30    Closing                154,147.89                     0.00

    =======================================================================
```

STUDENT DOCUMENTS
FOR THE END OF THE SECOND QUARTER, JUNE 30, 1997

Wild Goose Marina, Incorporated
Post Closing Trial Balance
June 30, 1997

	Accounts	Debit	Credit
101	Cash	$ 174,707.65	
102	Petty Cash	100.00	
103	Short-Term Investments	119,999.50	
105	Accounts Receivable	79,969.76	
106	Allowance for Doubtful Accounts		$ 2,475.00
109	Notes Receivable	221,500.00	
113	Interest Receivable	2,780.76	
116	Subscriptions Rec., Common Stock	92,400.00	
117	Merch. Inventory--Houseboats	785,330.00	
119	Merch. Inventory--Access.& Parts	34,200.00	
123	Prepaid Insurance	14,775.00	
124	Prepaid Rent	12,000.00	
127	Prepaid Advertising	235.00	
129	Office Supplies	549.50	
131	Service & Shop Supplies	1,441.13	
140	Invest. in Baldwin Manufacturing	218,509.70	
141	Long-Term Investments	1,255,955.50	
145	Service & Shop Equipment	231,365.00	
146	Accum. Dep., Serv. & Shop Equip.		35,705.00
149	Trucks	62,850.00	
150	Accum. Depreciation, Trucks		5,652.00
153	Trailers	65,000.00	
154	Accum. Depreciation, Trailers		7,500.00
157	Office Equipment	12,010.00	
158	Accum. Deprec., Office Equip.		4,240.00
160	Leasehold	174,375.00	
165	Leasehold Improvements	389,843.75	
170	Patents	2,981.25	
175	Organization Costs	5,625.00	
201	Accounts Payable		198,215.30
202	Interest Payable		1,273.34
203	Short-Term Notes Payable		270,000.00
204	Disc. on Short-Term Notes Pay.	2,957.78	
209	Salaries & Wages Payable		42,506.43
211	Sales Tax Payable		18,216.66
212	Estimated Property Taxes Payable		630.00
213	Income Taxes Payable		956.00
215	Unearned Moorage Fees		38,825.00
221	Employee's Federal Inc. Taxes Pay.		7,444.55
223	FICA Taxes Payable		8,275.58
225	State Unemployment Taxes Payable		555.22
227	Federal Unemployment Taxes Payable		185.07
235	Long-Term Lease Liability		6,000.00
236	Discount on Lease Financing	871.12	
241	Long-Term Notes Payable		105,000.00
242	Disc. on Long-Term Notes Pay.	7,967.50	
250	Bonds Payable		400,000.00
251	Discount on Bonds Payable	16,228.00	

Continued on next page

STUDENT DOCUMENTS
FOR THE END OF THE SECOND QUARTER, JUNE 30, 1997

Continued from previous page

	Accounts	Debit	Credit
301	Preferred Stock		100,000.00
303	Contrib. Cap. in Exc. of Par, Pref.		10,000.00
304	Contrib. Cap.--Retirement of Pref.		1,250.00
305	Common Stock		2,323,000.00
306	Common Stock Subscribed		100,000.00
308	Contrib. Cap. in Exc. of Par, Com.		117,515.00
315	Retained Earnings		208,157.75
330	Treasury Stock	27,050.00	
	Totals	$4,013,577.90	$4,013,577.90

STUDENT DOCUMENTS
FOR THE END OF THE SECOND QUARTER, JUNE 30, 1997

General Journal Entries

June 30	Houseboat Sales	401	1,253,777.78	
	Accessories & Parts Sales	407	41,310.00	
	Service Fees Earned	412	58,869.56	
	Moorage Fees Earned	415	50,250.00	
	Sales Commissions Earned	420	21,945.00	
	Purchases Discounts--Houseboats	502	21,890.00	
	Purch. Ret. & Allow.--Acc. & Parts	506	1,225.00	
	Purch. Discounts--Access. & Parts	507	633.95	
	Interest Earned	711	10,532.13	
	Dividends Earned	713	6,432.00	
	Earnings on Investments	715	16,950.00	
	Gain on Sale of Assets	721	3,325.00	
	Gain on Short-Term Investments	731	10,957.00	
	Miscellaneous Revenue	741	76.00	
	Income Summary	901	463,198.00	
	Income Summary	901		1,961,371.42

Closing Entry

STUDENT DOCUMENTS
FOR THE END OF THE SECOND QUARTER, JUNE 30, 1997

Date	Account	Acct #	Debit	Credit
June 30	Income Summary	901	1,807,223.53	
	Access. & Parts Sales Ret. & Allow.	408		370.00
	Purchases--Houseboats	501		1,456,000.00
	Transportation-In--Houseboats	503		37,230.00
	Purchases--Accessories & Parts	505		21,967.29
	Transportation-In--Access. & Parts	508		320.00
	Office & Shop Salaries & Wages Exp.	601		106,188.77
	Executive & Salespersons Salaries	602		54,000.00
	Rent Expense	603		27,781.25
	Equipment Rental Expense	604		4,500.00
	Office Supplies Expense	605		1,082.97
	Service & Shop Supplies Expense	606		1,413.75
	Truck Operating Expense	607		3,103.80
	Advertising Expense	608		2,508.75
	Credit Card Expense	609		196.21
	Delivery Expense	610		96.17
	Tools Expense	611		197.08
	Deprec. Exp., Serv. & Shop Equip.	613		5,780.00
	Deprec. Expense, Trucks	615		2,452.00
	Deprec. Expense, Trailers	617		1,500.00
	Deprec. Expense, Office Equipment	619		1,295.00
	Payroll Tax Expense	621		4,507.23
	Insurance Expense	622		6,875.00
	Bad Debt Expense	623		2,271.00
	Property Tax Expense	624		630.00
	Electric & Gas Expense	625		1,847.50
	Telephone Expense	626		1,403.70
	Bank Service Charges	627		61.00
	Cash Short and Over	628		8.00
	License Expense	629		1,407.50
	Professional Services Expense	630		1,440.00
	Janitorial Services Expense	631		966.50
	Amortization Expense--Patents	632		198.75
	Amortiz. Expense--Organiz. Costs	633		375.00
	Miscellaneous Expense	635		91.62
	Income Taxes Expense	811		32,456.00
	Interest Expense	813		19,037.72
	Loss on Sale/Disposal of Assets	821		250.00
	Loss on Retirement of Bonds	825		1,679.97
	Loss on Short-Term Investments	831		2,529.00
	Loss on Long-Term Investments	835		1,205.00
	Closing Entry			
June 30	Income Summary	901	154,147.89	
	Retained Earnings	315		154,147.89
	Closing Entry			
June 30	Retained Earnings	315	26,000.00	
	Cash Dividends Declared	320		26,000.00
	Closing Entry			

STUDENT DOCUMENTS
FOR THE END OF THE SECOND QUARTER, JUNE 30, 1997

General Journal Entries

June 30	Retained Earnings	315	30,015.00	
	Stock Dividends Declared	325		30,015.00
	Closing Entry			

FINAL EVALUATION

WILD GOOSE MARINA, INC.

June 30, 1997

FINAL EVALUATION   NAME_____

WILD GOOSE MARINA, INCORPORATED   SECTION_____DATE_____

1. How much cash was paid out on June 19? $ 91,200.00

2-3. Check number **04022** was issued to the Department of Motor
    Vehicles. On what date was this check issued and what   Date June 22
    was the number of the invoice paid in full?
                                                                Invoice Number DMV06

4. What is the reason for the June 28 debit entry
    to the Cash account?   Borrowed Cash--Note Payable

5. Over the next three years the balance of the Discount on Lease
    Financing account will be periodically amortized to what account?   Interest Expense

6. What is the Income From Operations for the quarter? $ 163,033.45

Remember that for all percentage questions your answers must be rounded to two decimal positions (4.57689% = 4.58%).

Total Net Revenues for the quarter ended June 30, 1997, total $1,425,782.34.

7. Service Fees, Moorage Fees, and Sales Commissions Earned are
    what percent of the total Net Revenues?   10.12%

8. Office & Shop Salaries and Wages Expense is what percent of total
    Operating Expenses?   45.35%

9. Office & Shop Salaries & Wages Expense combined with Executive
    & Salespersons Salaries are what percent of the total Net Revenues?   12.37%

10. Advertising Expense is what percent of total Operating Expenses?   1.07%

11. After income taxes, what other Other Expense account has the
    largest balance?   Interest Expense

12. If more efficient operation of the business had allowed management
    to reduce operating expenses 2%, what would have been the Income from
    Operations for the quarter? $ 167,717.02

13. If office and shop salaries and wages had been reduced 10% and all
    other **non-salary operating expenses** reduced 1%, how much would the
    Income from Operations have increased? $ 11,358.78

FINAL EVALUATION
WILD GOOSE MARINA, INCORPORATED

14-19. *CALCULATE the Cost of Good Sold for the Houseboats and Accessories & Parts on the form provided.*

```
                    Wild Goose Marina, Incorporated
                           Cost of Goods Sold
                    For Quarter Ended, June 30, 1997
---------------------------------------------------------------------------
  Houseboats

     Beginning Inventory, April 1, 1997...................$   315,200.00
     Purchases of Houseboats.......... $1,456,000.00
     Purchases Discounts--Houseboats..     21,890.00
                                       ---------------
     Net Purchases--Houseboats........  1,434,110.00 (14)
     Transportation-In--Houseboats....     37,230.00
                                       ---------------
     Cost of Purchases--Houseboats.........................  1,471,340.00 (15)
                                                            ------------
     Cost of Goods Available for Sale--Houseboats........$1,786,540.00
     Ending Inventory, June 30, 1997......................    785,330.00
                                                            ------------
        Cost of Goods Sold--Houseboats....................$1,001,210.00 (16)
                                                            ============

  Accessories & Parts

     Beginning Inventory, April 1, 1997................... $    41,132.00
     Purchases of Access. & Parts..... $    21,967.29
     Purch. Ret. & All.--Acc. & Parts. (    1,225.00)
     Purchases Discounts--Acc. & Parts (      633.95)
                                       ---------------
     Net Purchases--Access. & Parts... $    20,108.34 (17)
     Transport.-In--Access. & Parts...        320.00
                                       ---------------
     Cost of Purchases--Accessories & Parts...............      20,428.34 (18)
                                                            ------------
     Cost of Goods Available for Sale--Access. & Parts... $    61,560.34
     Ending Inventory, June 30, 1997......................      34,200.00
                                                            ------------
        Cost of Goods Sold--Accessories & Parts.......... $    27,360.34 (19)
                                                            ============
```

* *

FINAL EVALUATION
WILD GOOSE MARINA, INCORPORATED

20. The combined transportation-in costs for houseboats and accessories & parts total? **$37,550.00**

21. If 25% of the discounts on houseboat purchases had not been taken this quarter, how much of an increase would there have been in the cost of goods sold--houseboats? **$5,472.50**

22. The Gross Margin for houseboats is what percent of houseboat sales? **20.14%**

23. The Gross Margin for accessories & parts is what percent of total net accessories & parts sales? **33.17%**

24. Income from Operations is what percent of total Net Revenues? **12.59%**

25. Cost of Goods Sold--Houseboats is what percent of Houseboat Sales? **79.86%**

26. Executive & Salespersons Salaries are what percent of total Operating Expenses? **23.06%**

27. Total Operating Expenses are what percent of total Net Revenues? **18.09%**

28. What percentage of net income can be attributed to the gain on short-term investments? **7.11%**

29. What is the value of net Accounts Receivable? **$ 77,494.76**

30. What is the book value of the Service & Shop Equipment? **$ 195,660.00**

31. What is the total accumulated depreciation to date on the Trailers? **$ 7,500.00**

32. How much has the Investment In Baldwin Manufacturing changed this month (June)? **$10,950.00**

33. What is the current ratio? **2.63**

34. What is the acid-test (quick) ratio? Include Cash, Short-Term Investments, Accounts Receivable, Notes Receivable and Interest Receivable in your calculation. **1.02**

35. Does Wild Goose Marina, Inc., have enough cash on hand to meet current liabilities? YES   NO **X**

36. What is the June 30 working capital? **$ 953,387.93**

37. What is the total debt to total equity ratio (percentage)? **24.42%**

38. What is the return on common stockholder's equity (ending) for the quarter? Use Net Income and assume the quarterly preferred cash dividend totals $2,500. **5.55%**

FINAL EVALUATION
WILD GOOSE MARINA, INCORPORATED

39. Using average inventory, calculate the inventory turnover for the quarter. — **1.75**

40. Calculate the times fixed interest charges are earned. (Use income before interest and taxes) — **10.80**

41. What is the carrying value of the Long-Term Lease Liability? — **$ 5,128.88**

42. What is the carrying value of Long-Term Notes Payable? — **$ 57,032.50**

43. If Wild Goose Marina, Inc., has 23,230 shares of stock outstanding, what is the earnings per share (on Net Income) for the quarter? The preferred cash dividend for the quarter totals $2,500. — **$ 6.53**

44. Assuming that Preferred Stock is non-cumulative and non-participating, What is the equity per share for common stock? — **$ 117.64**

45. What is the total contributed capital from common stock? — **$ 2,540,515.00**

46. What is the total contributed capital from treasury stock? — **$ 0.00**

47. After closing, what is the balance of the Income Summary account? — **$ 0.00**

48. What is the reason for the "other deduction" item that appears on the on the Retained Earnings statement? — **Selling Treasury Stock At Less Than Cost**

49. What is the net increase in Retained Earnings this quarter? — **$ 97,432.89**

50. If, at the end of the quarter, the Retained Earnings account had a deficit balance of $50,000, what would be the total stockholders' equity of the company? — **$ 2,574,715.00**

51. Is the lease payment on June 30 for a capital (financing) lease or an operating lease? — **Capital**

52. How much investment is "tied up" in the leasehold and leasehold improvements? — **$ 564,218.75**

53-54. Identify by name the two customers who have past-due accounts. Remember that Wild Goose Marina, Inc., extends 30-day credit to all customers. — **Customer Bettencourt** / **Customer Corsetti**

55. Assuming all past-due accounts will be paid in the first five days of July, how much cash from accounts receivable should be collected during the first 15 days of July? — **$ 66,544.76**

56. Assuming no additional charges, how much cash will be needed for accounts payable obligations the first 15 days of July? — **$ 11,037.97**

FINAL EVALUATION
WILD GOOSE MARINA, INCORPORATED

57.	How much cash will be paid to Yee & Associates on or before July 30?	<u>$ 6,797.69</u>
58.	If the Corr Marine Supply account had not been paid on time, how much would this error have increased the cost of goods sold?	<u>$ 136.50</u>
59.	On June 28, Wild Goose Marina issued a $110,000 note payable at a discount. What is the **effective rate of interest** on this note.	<u>11.31%</u>
60.	If the June 28 note ($110,000) had been a **loan** at 8% interest that required four equal annual payments that <u>included interest</u>, what would be the amount of a single payment? (Table B)	<u>$ 33,211.56</u>
61.	If the note on June 28 ($110,000) had been a **loan** at 8% interest that required four equal annual payments <u>plus interest</u> on the unpaid balance, what would be the amount of the second payment?	<u>$34,100.00</u>
62-63.	What was the dollar increase and the percentage increase in total merchandise inventory from May 31 to June 30?	<u>$ 463,198.00</u> <u>129.99%</u>
64.	On June 1, Wild Goose Marina, Inc., retired a $200,000, 12%, 4-year bond issue (Series One Bonds) that provided the bond holders with an annual yield of 11%. On June 15, the company issued $400,000, 7%, 5-year bonds (Series One Bonds) that provided the bondholders with an annual yield of 8%. Assuming the bonds sold on June 15 for $200,000 instead of $400,000, what would be the net cost avoidance in interest paid, per quarterly interest period?	<u>$ 2,500.00</u>
65.	On June 30, Wild Goose Marina, Inc., received a $6,000 dividend check from Baldwin Manufacturing. The investment in Baldwin Manufacturing is accounted for under the "equity method." If the investment was accounted for under the "cost method", what account would be credited for the $6,000?	<u>**Dividends Earned**</u>

Wild Goose Marina, Inc.

OPTIONAL PROBLEMS

OPTIONAL PROBLEM A

Statement of Cash Flows

List in chronological order the **investing** activities that would be reported on a **Statement of Cash Flows**, for the month of June only. Show uses of cash from **investing** activities with brackets.
*Notes Receivable from customers are considered to be operating activities.

	Date	Investing Activities	Provided or Used
1.	6/9	Sale of Investment in Folsom Corporation	$ 28,682.50
2.	6/10	Sale of office equipment	350.00
3.	6/15	Extraordinary repair	(9,550.00)
4.	6/16	Stock investment in SunKraft Houseboats	(5,955.50)
5.	6/17	Sale of service and shop equipment	2,600.00
6.	6/22	Purchase of a truck	(30,000.00)
7.	6/22	Leasehold improvements	(75,000.00)
8.	6/26	Purchase of a forklift	(37,200.00)
9.	6/30	Sale of investment	1,698.00
10.	6/30	Investment in Baldwin Manufacturing	6,000.00
		Total Cash Provided or (Used) by Investing Activities	($ 118,375.00)

List in chronological order the **financing** activities that would be reported on a **Statement of Cash Flows**, for the month of June only. Show uses of cash from **financing** activities with brackets.

	Date	Financing Activities	Provided or Used
1.	6/2	Retirement of Folsom Corporation bonds	($ 206,000.00)
2.	6/5	Cash dividends paid	(25,600.00)
3.	6/8	Collection from stock subscriptions	122,250.00
4.	6/8	Sale of common stock	128,500.00
5.	6/12	Purchase of treasury stock	(40,575.00)

OPTIONAL PROBLEM A (continued)

6.	**6/15**	**Sale of bonds**	**$ 383,659.80**
7.	**6/17**	**Sale of treasury stock**	**12,825.00**
8.	**6/19**	**Collection from stock subscriptions**	**39,600.00**
9.	**6/19**	**Payment of short-term note**	**(90,000.00)**
10.	**6/28**	**Issue a note payable**	**106,975.00**
11.	**6/30**	**Payment of long-term note**	**(12,362.50)**
12.	**6/30**	**Payment on long-term lease liability**	**(500.00)**
13.	**6/30**	**Retirement of preferred stock**	**(108,750.00)**

Total Cash Provided or (Used) by Financing Activities   **$ 309,662.30**

14. By examining the beginning and ending Cash account balance and the findings above for the cash provided or used by investing and financing activities, determine the amount of cash used by operating activities during the month of June.   **$ 242,254.88**

15-16. What was the single, largest amount of cash used by operating activities and on what date did it occur?   **$ 419,810.00**

    Date June 27

17. If the investing activities of June 22, and June 26 had not occurred, what would have been the net cash provided or (used) by investing activities during the month of June?   **$ 23,825.00**

18. What financing activity provided the single largest amount of cash?

    Sale of Bonds

19. If the financing activity that provided the largest amount of Cash had not occurred, what would have been the amount of the ending balance in the cash account on June 30? (Indicate a credit balance with brackets.)   **($ 208,952.15)**

20. What investing activity used the single largest amount of cash?

    Leasehold Improvements

OPTIONAL PROBLEM B

Bond Sinking Fund Schedule

On June 15, 1997, Wild Goose Marina, Inc., issued $400,000 in Series Two, 7%, 5-year Bonds. Assume that an annual bond sinking fund deposit is required at the end of each year with the first deposit being made June 15, 1998. Using Table C in the appendix, complete the sinking fund bond schedule shown below.

```
                    Wild Goose Marina, Incorporated
                         Sinking Fund Schedule
                           Series Two Bonds
```

Issue Date: June 15, 1997
Bond Par Value: $400,000.00
Periods of Fund Deposits: 5
Sinking Fund Interest Rate: 5.50%

Annual Deposits Required: | $71,680.00 |

End of Year	Amount Deposited	Interest Earned on Fund Balance	Balance in Fund After Deposit and Interest
June 15, 1998	$71,680.00	$0.00	$71,680.00
June 15, 1999	$71,680.00	$3,942.40	$147,302.40
June 15, 2000	$71,680.00	$8,101.63	$227,084.03
June 15, 2001	$71,680.00	$12,489.62	$311,253.65
June 15, 2002	$71,680.00	$17,118.95	$400,052.60

1. How much interest will be earned on sinking fund investments from June 15, 1998, until June 15, 1999, assuming the fund will earn the estimated 5.5 percent interest? $ 0.00

2. How much interest will be earned on sinking fund investments from June 15, 1999, until June 15, 2000, assuming the fund will earn 5.5 percent interest? $ 3,942.40

3. If the sinking fund final balance is greater than $400,000, what account will be debited for the excess? Cash

4. Over the five-year period, how much cash will actually be deposited by Wild Goose Marina, Inc., into the account? $ 358,400.00

OPTIONAL PROBLEM C

Depreciation Schedule--Truck

On June 22, 1997, Wild Goose Marina, Inc., acquired, on a trade, a new truck for use in the business operations. The truck cost $32,850, has an estimated salvage value of $2,850, and an estimated 4-year useful life. Assuming that the depreciation will be recorded on an annual basis, complete the four-year truck depreciation schedule shown below. Use your data to answer the questions presented.

```
              Wild Goose Marina, Incorporated
                    Depreciation Schedule
                            Truck

Acquired:        June 22, 1997
Asset Cost:      $32,850.00
Salvage Value:   $2,850.00
Life in Years:        4
```

			Depreciation Expense	
Time Period	Year	Straight-Line	Sum-of-The-Year's Digits	Declining Balance
1	1997	$3,750.00	$6,000.00	$8,212.50
2	1998	$7,500.00	$10,500.00	$12,318.75
3	1999	$7,500.00	$7,500.00	$6,159.38
4	2000	$7,500.00	$4,500.00	$3,079.69
Totals		$26,250.00	$28,500.00	$29,770.31

1. Assuming straight-line depreciation is used, what will be the book value of the truck on December 31, 1998? $ 21,600.00

2. If Sum-of-the-Years-Digits depreciation is used, what will be the total accumulated depreciation on the truck on December 31, 1999? $ 24,000.00

3. If declining balance depreciation is used for the truck, what will be the book value of the truck on December 31, 1997? $24,637.50

4. Using declining balance depreciation, what will be the total acculmulated depreciation on the truck on December 31, 2000? $29,770.31

OPTIONAL PROBLEM D

Depreciation Schedule
Service and Shop Equipment--Forklift

On June 26, 1997, Wild Goose Marina, Inc., acquired, on a trade, a new forklift for use in the business service operations. Assuming that the depreciation will be recorded on **a quarterly basis**, complete the forklift depreciation schedule shown below. Compute the depreciation expense for only the <u>first five quarters</u>. Use your data to answer the questions presented.

```
            Wild Goose Marina, Incorporated
                  Depreciation Schedule
            Service and Shop Equipment - Forklift
```

Acquired: June 26, 1997

Asset Cost: | $39,520.00 |

Salvage: $4,520.00
Life in Years: 5

Depreciation Expense

Qtr.	Year	Straight-Line	Sum-of-The-Year's Digits	Declining Balance
3rd	1997	$1,750.00	$2,916.67	$1,976.00
4th	1997	$1,750.00	$2,916.67	$1,877.20
1st	1998	$1,750.00	$2,916.67	$1,783.34
2nd	1998	$1,750.00	$2,916.67	$1,694.17
3rd	1998	$1,750.00	$2,333.33	$1,609.46

1. Assuming straight-line depreciation is used, what will be the book value of the forklift at the end of 1997?   <u>$ 37,770.00</u>

2. If declining balance depreciation is used, what will be the book value of the forklift on June 30, 1998?   <u>$ 32,189.29</u>

3. If sum-of-the-years-digits depreciation is used, will there be depreciation expense recorded on the forklift for 2002?   <u>YES   X NO</u>

4. If units-of-production depreciation was used for the forklift, is it possible that depreciation expense could be recorded on this asset during 2003?   <u>YES   X NO</u>